QUENTIN ROWAN was born in New York City in 1976. His first novel, *Assassin of Secrets*, published under the name Q.R. Markham, was withdrawn shortly after publication when it was discovered to consist almost entirely of passages plagiarized from a wide variety of sources. Subsequently, earlier short stories of his that had appeared in *The Paris Review*, *BOMB Magazine*, and elsewhere proved to be largely plagiarized as well.

PRAISE, PRAISE, AND EVEN MORE PRAISE FROM THE INTERNET AND NEWSPAPERS FOR QUENTIN ROWAN

"[*Never Say Goodbye*] is written in highly stylized, often grandiose language."
– *THE NEW YORKER*

"The reason that Quentin's book [*Assassin of Secrets*] makes everyone so nervous and aggrieved is that it reminds us of the vast gray area that we all occupy."
– JONATHAN LETHEM

"I doubt he'll get a real chance unless he writes under a nom de plume – which, I suppose, could become his new addiction: he'll claim he was addicted to shape-shifting into new literary identities when he's outed for that."
– REX PICKETT

"As for the idiot who's the focus of this article, I think he's exactly that: an idiot. And I find it disheartening that a thief gets all of this attention while so many authors who, you know, create things, are largely ignored."
– ROBERT BROWNE

"Everyone deserves a second chance, but pardon my skepticism. It just doesn't seem like an auspicious new beginning when someone whom people call a plagiarist pens an apology that rings so very false."
– MARY ELIZABETH WILLIAMS

"Oh, right. Jackass."
– MEG GARDINER

"Nobody's going to publish you anyway now."
– JEREMY DUNS

"In other news, it's becoming clear that Quentin Rowan, perpetrator of this delicious fraud, is merely a sad little con."
– CHAUNCEY MABE

"If Rowan has any sense, he will completely disappear from the literary stage and never again, as Markham or as Rowan, try to publish his writing professionally."
– PAUL CONSTANT

"In the hundreds of newspaper articles and blog posts that have been published on the subject of Markhamgate in the past twenty-four hours, one question appears over and over: How did Rowan think he'd get away with this, especially in the era of Google?"
– MACY HALFORD

"This guy deserves to be a night manager at a Wendy's. He deserves to NEVER be able to sell his work to a publisher again . . . I hope he gets run over by a truck."
– *THE BULLSHIT FIGHTER*

"This isn't really the right blog for this catchphrase, but Christ, what an asshole."
– MJFGATES

"The guy is a talentless thief who deserves to be hauled up in front of his peers and [made to] account for his abhorrent actions."
– SIMON GARDNER

"Being addicted to bad decisions is not a disease. It's just being a douche weasel."
– JOHN CLARK

"I think people should take this asswipe as a cautionary tale."
– JON HANSEN

"Thanks for exposing Quentin Rowan's noxious self-justification. He reminds [me] of those murder defendants at sentencing hearings who say "I wish I could take it back," "I wish I could give my life for hers," etc. – just as sincere, and just as hollow."
– PETER ROSOVSKY

"You could've called it the world's first "book mashup" and gotten front-page coverage in *VICE*, you hipster douchebag."
– JEREMY MEYERS

Probably no significance, but is that guy trying to look like Carlos the Jackal?
– CAPTAIN TIGHTPANTS

"He might have such thick skin [that this won't] bother him. But at least he'll always be a really ugly ****."
– DAVID SCHOFIELD

"If you see this guy, chop his fingers off."
– *BLOOD SWEAT AND MURDER*

"I see through your bullshit, Quentin Rowan, and I'm not happy. It doesn't matter if your literary novels do sell afterwards, because of your scheme. You're a cheater and you're no better than any writer."
– BENOIT LELIEVRE

"This is epic. Biblical. The poor fucking . . . idiot."
– SIMON

"Come on, Rowan. You can 'write' another book – we'll be more interested the second time round. Now you've gone glamorising yourself, with your sleazy behavior. We want more, Rowan. Write us a dirty book. We're asking for it."
– JOE MCCANN

"You are awful. Hit your fucking knees, and ask God to forgive you."
– ERIK SWANSON

"Quentin, I live here in Brooklyn and I'm a writer and I'm telling you right now – I'm scouring the hipster dutchbag bars and hirsute coffee lounges for as long as it takes to find you, and when I do . . . I'm going to grind your bones to make my bread."
– TIMOTHY READY

"'People-pleasing?' Hardly. If you don't feel capable of writing, why in the world are you trying to sell a novel? What were you going to do for an encore – lift the combined works of Shakespeare and his contemporaries?"
– C. ANDREW WOLFE

"S.T.F.U., you pomo hipster pseudo-intellectual."
– LEAH RAEDER

"Don't care to read anything 'written' by this twat."
– PECKSIE

"I look forward to your next attempt to spin your theft into a cry for pity. Scum."
– CURT

"And to the prick who thought he could get away with it: piss off, and let real writers have a go at telling original stories, will you? There's a good lad."
– *ALARMING*

"Anyone else think that he looks like a fat John Lennon?"
– *MULLETS*

"Occam's razor: he's just a douche."
– SIRKOWSKI

"The poor dumb bastard didn't just shoot himself in the foot on this one, he emptied the clip and reloaded, and there seem to be even more rounds left."

– BRYCE

"Odds are I could just hand him the gun and at this point, he'd do it himself."

– COMMANDER RNVR

"Hit 'like' if you think that Markham looks like a fat John Lennon."

– JIM

"What a maroon, what an all-day sucker."

– TURAFISH

"Mr. Rowan's self-serving list of excuses takes passive-aggressive douchebaggery to a whole new level."

– ROB

"Pay back the advance, and shut up Q.R. You are not a fat Lennon, you are a fat Chapman."

– PETER B.

"Waaaaaah! Cry me a river, fuck face."

– JOSH

"Rowan is a total and complete dipshit."

– STERN J.

"And there's nothing hip about this four-eyed meatloaf."

– POWERS BOOTHE

"Quentin Rowan. Who in the hell does that to a defenseless infant?"

– CAT BALLOU

Never Say Goodbye

A MEMOIR

Quentin Rowan

Illustrations by Josh Bayer

Yeti
VERSE CHORUS PRESS

YETI books are published by Verse Chorus Press
for Yeti Publishing, PO Box 14806, Portland OR 97293.
yetipublishing.com

Illustrations © 2012 Josh Bayer (joshbayer.com)
Cover collage by Rachel Day (rachelbethday.com)
Cover scan by Gilbert Plantinga (gpphotographics.com)
Book design by Steve Connell/Transgraphic (transgraphic.net)

Library of Congress Cataloging-in-Publication Data

Rowan, Quentin, 1976-
Never say goodbye : a memoir / by Quentin Rowan.
p. cm.
ISBN 978-1-891241-58-1 (pbk.)—ISBN 978-1-891241-91-8 (ebook)
1. Rowan, Quentin—Childhood and youth. 2. Authors, American—21st century—Biography. 3. Plagiarism—United States—History—21st century. I. Title.
PS3613.A7542Z46 2012
813'.6--dc23
[B]

2012020085

NEVER SAY GOODBYE

1

To my dear friend J:

As much as I miss you, I am glad that you are not here to see me now. I did something wrong, and the world laughed and pointed fingers and sent me to that island again. The one where shame blows in from the sea, green and smooth and reflective like glass, where they send child dictators who have overreached themselves? You were not only the first person I stole from but also the first person to forgive me. You would be thirty-five this year, married, and working as a scientist in Chicago. I write this confession for you, J, from my island perch.

CHAPTER ONE

(birth canal, C-section, pink and fuzzy, rain over the East River, Winston Churchill, vermicelli, crying like an Irishman for his whiskey)

We were the sons of single mothers, and though I never properly knew what happened to J's father, mine had moved several blocks southeast after the divorce. From Seventh and Seventh, our humble block where the Edelmans and the Whites and the Bogers lived, where I did gymnastics on the old lead pipe outside the creamsicle-striped deli, to Eighth and Eleventh, by the rusty-fronted laundromat near the Irish boys club. My father would take me there and play me records by Grand Funk Railroad and Beethoven, and I'd jump up and down on the gingernut bed till my head was light, yelling, "Bad Beethoven! Bad Beethoven!" then fall asleep after canned soup and Saltines.

He was trying not to drink and had left his old teaching job at the Quaker school to become a banker at a big bank on Park Avenue. He was going to AA meetings and only saw me on weekends. When I looked up at him or asked him to carry me, he seemed like the tallest thing on this one-clouded earth, with a mess of fine-smelling brown hair and turtle-shell glasses. Holding me close to his cheek I could feel the slight blue stubble press against me, and I knew I was safe in some reckless way.

Not home, but safe.

When I asked him to tell the red-haired girl with the see-through skin across Eighth Avenue that I loved her, he suggested I do it myself. It was a very serious thing to say.

My mother would pick me up, sometimes with a stroller because she complained I walked too slowly, distracted by a leaf or a fat clump pie of mulberries on the road. I remember some of the sidewalk was grouted and chalky, broken up like a medieval staircase, and other parts were clean and smooth like the future. Brownstones were the streets, mostly, with an old, low, brick condominium here and there.

Our next-door neighbors, the Dineens, an old Irish couple, would chat with me through the metal wicket fence in our backyard, and there were always nannies: Mrs. Bartley, and the other one I picked up the Brooklyn accent from, and who was promptly fired for it.

The light in the late seventies was different and came slanty through the shutters and bars on my window. Bars on my crib, and maybe things that lived beneath. They were there to keep me in.

Furniture was made of bars, straight lines and curved. Smooth wood or graphlike fabrics. My father left the house after his third suicide attempt. He was dry, on Antabuse, and tried to slit his wrists in an overcoat. The overcoat, so I wouldn't have to see the blood if I was crawling around somewhere.

My mother loved him so much that she stayed with him through two self-induced comas. I understood why she loved him so much: his funny laugh, his thoughtful pauses, his way of thinking which traveled through the crevices of the ordinary.

But they took him to a place where the doctors were zapping people.

And then she told him he couldn't come back.

My mother's face was long and lightish brown like a Cherokee's. Her long dark hair fell down over her ears to her shoulders, which in those days were mostly covered by a turtleneck or a dashiki. She wore very light blue jeans and Stan Smiths on her feet.

I had always nannies so she had time to paint. Photo-realist still lifes, where every ripple in the blue fabric and every crumb from the yellow loaf spotted your eyes like threaded water.

*****

In the morning we would walk all the way down Prospect Park West, where it was dense with statues of generals and other great men I'd never heard of, who'd fought in wars I'd never heard of, which seemed to say to a young boy that being this thing, Man, meant growing a mustache and wearing a big-brimmed hat. It meant sacrifice, perhaps even that of your best horse. Because you see, there were affairs about in the world, and men with mustaches were the shapers of these clouds.

Elm trees, mulberries, lindens, and sycamore, dank and loose-leafed, ran down in T-squares from the park and playground, shrouding the windows of houses that had once belonged to Irish and Italians, who had been fine builders and craftsmen but too light in the purse to stay long, after all, in that green world.

The daughters of Bryn Mawr and Radcliffe, Grosse Pointe and Shaker Heights had set their sights on this place the other side of the river and south, so far south of Claremont Avenue and Riverside Drive. We were their children: fruit of the loins of the first generation of Americans to have known only the comfort and revolt of the postwar years and the Great Society.

And we all went to preschool together at a place called the Children's Center.

Maureen and Paul were the names of our minders, and they paid special mind to me because, as people would later say, I had no skin. There was no thickness to it and everyone knew.

Deep in the panther dark of naptimes, death threats were made upon my person by a young bruiser named Ben and his crony.

And fear, which was not yet the fear of life, was one of my first great sensations.

To my aid came only Spider-Man. Gazing back into the child-plump and air-blue eyes of the bullies, he and I became one in mind if not body and, gilded with fear and sleep, I'd shoot imaginary webs around them. We were Quaker and I could not fight, so the cerebral webs were the only ones I had, and though they were effective enough in preschool, they would prove to be inconsequential against the machinations of adults.

The death threats continued for years as the same group of kids all wound up at school and summer camp with me. I refused to go on a walk over the Brooklyn

Bridge because Ben had intimated that he'd throw me over the railing, and later, to Riis Park, where he had threatened to drown me in the green breast of the sea.

Safe with my toys and comic books was the mute knowledge that I could outsmart the bullies even if it meant playing sick and staying home.

Peter Parker was a smart guy after all, a science whiz who'd taken his fair share of knee-rattling from Flash Thompson. But by the time he'd got his super powers and designed his web shooters, he was too busy with real villains, the rattling death-breath and horror of adult villains like the Vulture and the Green Goblin, to take his revenge on dick-swingers like Flash lathering up in the shower before the big game.

Spider-Man was the silent man as portrayed on *The Electric Company*, the silent sufferer who swung through the death rays and smoke of bad people, cruel people, to help good ones.

My mother approved of my crush on Spider-Man, allowing me accessories that bore his mark. My favorite of all was a T-shirt some friends of hers brought back from Italy: *L'Uomo Ragno*. From then on, those words, *L'Uomo Ragno*, were a code between the two of us, a childhood incantation to rise above the clammy hands of villains both real and imaginary with silence and with dignity.

As language entered the picture and words flew fumblingly from my tongue, the other *Uomo*, the *Uomo* of Stan Lee and Steve Ditko who cracked wise at the dark forms of his enemies as he wound them in his measured webs, became a more fitting model. I was never at a loss for words, though in later years I'd learn rotten and I'd learn well to hold my tongue, in lessons meted out by serpents and dark crones on toadstools and common conquerors who had only fists, when it came to fighting children.

*****

My mother taught me language and spoke language with me until it rang in my brain. And I would say to her with my thick milk tongue: *Who chose this body for me, mama?* Who chose this mind? That I was never quite alive to and fit me funny.

She was dark with deep, speckled eyes, my father too, and their faces were pale with paradoxes while I was fair and my shoulders broad and everyone said I would become a football star one day.

The question was: could those shoulders save me or protect me from my own rogues gallery? Not the Goblin, or the Rhino, or Mysterio this time, but characters like the Masturbator Babysitter.

The one who sat bemused and firm, cock in hand, upon a stool in my mother's studio on the parlor floor and stared out the window, gazing northwards towards Methodist Hospital and the park, as he brought himself to fruition over and over. He had an unfresh face and a ratty teenage mustache like a junkyard skyline and was the son of some family down the block.

I would ask to be excused, to go to my own room to play alone but he wouldn't let me. Even though we had nothing to say to each other, I was forced to bear witness to his witless hormonal striving. I was his captive and that made his smile broad and his dick hard as he came, over

L'UOMO RAGNO
L'UOMO RAGNO

and over again on the parlor floor.

I sat there in that room on the other side of it and imagined I was Spider-Man in issue #33 trapped under tons of heavy machinery by the Master Planner. Aunt May was in the hospital wasting away because of a radioactive isotope in her blood. And it was all my fault, because I'd given her the transfusion. I'd fought the Lizard and torn apart the underworld looking for a cure, but found myself here, trapped by the new villain in town.

And as I struggled with all my strength, deep in a fifty-foot hole, for that bright, that clean instant when I could throw this burden off my shoulders, I thought: *I've got to free myself – No matter how impossible it seems . . . I'll get that serum to Aunt May! And maybe then I'll no longer be haunted by the memory – of Uncle Ben!*

I rose, and the Masturbator watched me guardedly. I said, "I need to get some water."

"Why?"

"I'm thirsty."

"Drink your own piss," he said.

*****

I was always falling in love with redheads with see-through skin. The second one's name was Emma. In kindergarten at the Quaker School, we struck up a deal to show each other some private parts. I went first and she screamed.

School was downtown on a little inlet called Adams: just starboard of a crummy park strewn with junkies and tons of those Greek coffee cups. Nearer was Jay Street with its pawn shops and placarded office buildings, with businesses like the kinds that advertised in the back pages of comic books. Beyond that, the courthouses where they took muggers and Mafia men from Carroll Gardens, and sometimes we went there for a passport too.

We grew into a pretty healthy gang of kids over time: J, me, Josh, Nate, Adam, Donald, and Danny. There was also the boy with the bladder problem and the bandage over his eye. And those Sikh kids with turbans from Atlantic Avenue.

J's hair was blond and his mother's red, and they were both gold-skinned. He was the automatist, the steady one of our group, and when I told him in his backyard that we were going to form a band, he replied pityingly that there wasn't time, what with soccer and school and breakdancing classes. I'd already written a song called "This Is the Day of Your Life," and I'd made drawings of us and where we'd stand on stage and so on, but when I tried to sing it for him there, out by the open-ribbed black metal fence in that clandestine green garden, he laughed.

"It's good, but it needs work," he said.

"I think it's good how it is."

"What does it mean? *The day of your life*? Every day is the day of your life."

J and I rarely fought, but when we did, when he held me in unsteady and uneager silence, it usually had to do with moral issues. On a school trip junket, all holding hands in a line to trickle like honey across some interface road, we fought about who was better, Michael Jackson or Weird Al. I preferred "Eat It," poor creature that I was, while J made that point that a *take-off*, as we used to call them, could never better the original.

"But it's funny," I said.

"It's stupid," he said.

"He sings just as good."

"No way."

"The words are funnier."

"That's not the point."

His hand grew limp in mine as I tried to explain the power of satire. Then he switched spots with someone else so he wouldn't have to hold my hand, and gave me grave looks the rest of the trip. But I was hyperkinetic as a boy, always changing my mind and going into quick trances over things like Weird Al or *Tron* or breakdancing, the turbulence of which brought us together again, to choreograph a dance in his bedroom that involved jumping off the bunkbed and blithering along the floor, as the afternoon light slid over our unprotected smiles.

I used to get so excited about these tangential things: I could see us forming our own breakdance crew or soccer team and running off from school, with its nameless weaknesses and smelly musk of clay and crayons. But J would keep me in check, axis back to first grade radii, reminding me our job was to be kids, kids who went to school and took naps and learned to read from fresh-faced teachers with a woven cross-flow of high-minded ideals.

To the rattle of rucksacks and the frequency of children singing "Beat It," I'd wonder about J's father and who he was and where he came from, or if it was J's mother who made J so particularly steady and loyal. There was something metered and complicated about J's parental situation, in its transience, that managed to make me all the more jealous of how self-contained he managed to be. I wanted something like that balance so badly myself but the green-sickness always came back, the shrill and nervy touch of thought and pain like invisible needles up and down my octopus mind.

Sitting alone in his J's room in the dribbling center of a gelatin spring afternoon, with J in the bathroom, I found something I wanted even more than his calm, his clear, clarifying calm. It was a toy, a Spider-Man figurine. And I stole it.

Why did I steal from my best friend?

A small avatar container for the childhood mess and the basic lack of power that sits with youth. Wishing I could funnel myself down to action-figure size. Safe to do battle with other plastic men. Safer than blood and flesh and cells and atoms all queasy in their livingness.

I know it is too late now to mean anything, but I stole from you, J.

And I am sorry.

THE BLACK HOLE
BLACK HOLE
BLACK HOLE
BLACK HOLE
BLACK HOLE
THE BLACK HOLE
BLACK HOL

CHAPTER TWO

(little boy in corduroys, spaghetti and cheese, life drawing class and vacuum cleaner, apostrophe, you got slapped, cheek to the carpet, deathless deathless)

Jocelyn, an African American woman my father met at AA and then married, had grown up in Crown Heights, where her father, Big Roscoe, had a construction business that was a front for the Mob. Her son Yasunari and I were fast friends, but he was always off somewhere riding his Big Wheel and leaving me alone with Roscoe and his wife, Juanita.

Taking a cigarette out and putting it in his mouth, Roscoe would tip his Kangol hat to me and say, "You gonna be a football player when you grow up?"

And I'd say, "Yep."

And he'd say, "What's your team?"

"Cowboys."

"The *Dallas* Cowboys?"

"Yeah."

"I bet you just like those cheerleaders. You some kinda little pervert?"

"I like the uniforms."

"Do you follow politics?"

"Only a little."

"Who you gonna vote for?"

"I'm only four and a half."

"Who you vote for if you *could*, little man?"

"Carter."

"Not *Reagan*?"

"I dunno."

"They say Jessie Jackson might run this year."

"Who's that?"

"Jessie Jackson gonna turn this country around. I know the man personally, and he going to put me on his staff when he gets elected."

"That's neat."

"What you drinking there?"

"Juice."

"Try some of this. Garlic water. It's good for your heart."

"Do I have to?"

"Just one sip, boy."

He handed me the glass carafe of lightly twinkling water. Cloves of garlic swam like white corpses in the liquid. And rather than drink it, I ran away, down the ruin of the pubic-carpeted stairs and through linoleum rooms of space and memory and the impatience of plastic-covered furniture to the kitchen, where Juanita slaved on wings of excess to make us all waffles, chicken, and collard greens.

I'd sit on a spinny chair to watch her, and she'd watch me watching and laugh maliciously.

"Boy, you always watching and watching, but you don't say nothing."

"Sorry."

"Don't say sorry. It's just no one knows what you're thinking when you like that."

"I was wondering, when is my dad coming back?"

"Well, he left you here with us till tomorrow, you know that. But you got your new brother now, don't you?"

"Un huh."

"You want a waffle?"

"Not right now. Thanks."

"You love your new brother, don't you?"

"Sure I do."

"Well that *is* sweet. Because the two of you . . . you my little boobies, you know that?"

A smile came to my boy's lips.

"*Boobies*?"

"You two my little boobies, and don't you forget it!"

"Is that like a booby trap?"

"Don't make me go setting no booby traps for my little boobies!"

With a quizzical crook of a grin, I went down the backstairs to the unwinning garden of mostly tomato plants and an occasional praying mantis, thinking: *Time is the destroyer*. Time is the great impaler.

Time is the father.

Who's floated away somewhere with the day to be with his strange woman in darkness. Time is the father who has left me. Here. Impaled. Far from any semblance of my own form.

Father is the destroyer.

And out in the alleyway there was my new brother riding his Big Wheel, smiling, eager for me to join him.

Closing my eyes and making the world go dark, I forced the gabble of a smile and joined him.

*****

I came to love Yasunari as a brother, but behind him always was the augury of his mother's shadow, tattooed on his back. When she was young she was beautiful like a four-letter word. But there was a darkness inside of her, a whispering pain that made her beat up on children.

It started with her taking the clothes off my back and putting them on Yas. My own mother never had any money and worked hard to buy nice clothes for me. At the time she was suffering from a serious thyroid condition, but Jocelyn didn't know that and I suppose the stealing was her way of scoring a point against my mother. It went on for several months until Jocelyn took the one thing I cared for most in this world: my *L'uomo Ragno* T-shirt.

That was when I realized webs weren't enough. To merely cast nets would be to welcome death from her fists, the dark language of the forcemeat of her flesh pulverizing my own.

One weekend my mother picked me up and Yas came down wearing my *L'Uomo Ragno* T-shirt. She tried to take it off his back for me, but my father wrestled with her for it over the grassy chains in Stuyvesant Town.

When my mother refused to send me there anymore, my father banned his new wife from stealing my clothes.

In response, she started locking me out of the apartment.

I'm sure it was spring because the air was warm on the peachy hair of my bare arms when she threw me into the hall and locked the door. The world was open like an operating room, all free and blue with normal families playing games and catching dog balls, and I was left to wander the streets of the Lower East Side looking for my dad.

*****

Cresting the whitewash infinite of the weekend wave was back to Brooklyn, Prospect Heights now, and my mother's new husband, Joe, who worked as a city planner on Court Street but carried home with him, if not in his briefcase then in his whole cogito, a kind of rigid map-making quality. Joe's children were Nick and Anna. His first wife had gone to National Cathedral School like my mother, but died tragically young. I remember her fleetingly, Libby. She was good and kind to me when I knew her.

He wasn't mean like Jocelyn, just distant. Neither he nor my mother tended to come down to our level very often, so we had to swim up to theirs, through their years of high school and Ivy League education, to be able to talk about the windows at Chartres rather than G.I. Joe and Strawberry Shortcake.

Nick was older with cool pale black hair; he kind of gave it all the finger and wore rock T-shirts. But Anna was my age, liony blonde with a gap in her front teeth, and she and I were young enough to want to impress. We found new ways, always, to express interest in Thatcher, the hostages in Iran, the latest issue of *Consumer Reports*, or Napoleon trapped on the island of Elba.

Whenever we came back to him, every few years, he was still there, I'm afraid.

Elba.

The place where child dictators went when they'd overreached themselves in the eyes of the *beau monde.* So we learned: these were the men who could keep you down. The ones who only wanted more of the same and would grab your tiny black-booted feet if you scrambled too high on their song-and-dance ramparts.

Elba.

Island of shame and the persistence of shame, where they buried people under its strata, the reign of its perfection, and told those same people to "get used to it." And to "cling to what you think you know."

"We know what is real on this island and its name is shame."

And the years moved, moon and sun and daffodils, through some kind of elliptical orbit themselves, bringing occasional quicksand smiles but mostly *Romper Room* and *Captain Kangaroo.*

My mother writes: *But have you really captured your childhood self? What about the fellow who played chess at Brooklyn Friends but never let on, so that when I went to the parents' evening and tried to guess the riddles, I could guess from "I have an elephant in my window." Not "I play chess."*

Art or the idea of art was presented to me at some point, perhaps by my mother, perhaps by some invisible committee in my head as the only redeemingly real kind of extension outward from the silent hours. Nick became an aspiring musician and Anna a talented thespian; I started attending art classes for gifted youngsters in Soho, when it was still Soho and not some strange Xanadu of blue-jeans emporiums.

That was the second time I stole.

The other kids were much older and certainly more talented. So I copied what the kid next to me was doing. My mind went blank and all I could see was that his drawing was better. He noticed what I was doing, told our instructor and she was very nice about it. Said something like all artists start out copying. A good artist is just an individual with a talent for mimicry, who can eventually turn that gift into something else.

What was odd to me was that I knew there was this parade of junk in my head, so naturally different from anyone else's that it seemed I'd be a natural when it came to this whole creativity rigamarole. But when it was pencil to paper time, everything went limp. Was it the boundary game? The moment the mind stuff was transfused to the page, the glimmer of it went out. Wasn't the same. Could not yet properly put the inside out.

Why was I being told I was talented anyway? Because I could do a good drawing of Spider-Man? I wasn't a tracer but I could look at a picture, all the lines and shadows, and recreate it. Couldn't do it an hour later, but it would stay in my head a few minutes.

I was a born copyist, I guess you could say, like Wyatt Gwyon, and though the second act of theft wasn't as painful because it wasn't from a friend, it strikes home a little more winningly, because it was an idea.

Not a thing.

*****

Every other Thursday Dad would pick me up early from school to see a movie or have pizza in the old centurion wastes of the Fulton Mall, where basketball sneakers lined the streets like some newfangled form of wampum. Follow Fulton's pedestrian walkway and you'd arrive at the Albee Square Mall, made famous by Biz Markee and the only place to buy an Orange Julius for miles around.

There was an old Loew's auditorium in the mall with loads of arcade games and nihilistic action films. I thought Stallone and Schwarzenegger were cool and all, but then they'd spray an entire beach with machine gun fire, and I'd think: Is that what it means to be a man?

My father writes: *Appreciated your mother's comment, where is Quentin? Sometimes I had the same reaction: where is the lively, kind, friendly, sensitive, bright, funny young man I love? I am reminded of your remarks on character: maybe what we have is our scattered perceptions and we need friends, lovers, confidants to explain us to us.*

Summer camp in Lakewood became a place to play at being a young man with the Jewish offspring of Scarsdale and Mamaroneck. The whole month of torture was a lead up to some kind of faux-Olympics of world domination. We were all given a primary color and separated from the kids we'd spent a month grudgingly getting to know. Suddenly they were our enemies, and we were simply red, blue, or yellow, and for a week our only goal was to annihilate them.

The really true fun thing about summer camp was lake swimming. These colonies of shiny fish that bit your nipples, everyone called them 'titty fish' and an old German instructor called the windsurfing simulator the *stimulator.* I loved the tranquil lukewarm lake in summer, but I had learned to swim in the ocean and it was no substitute for feeling the tide and the undertow frothing against you. Or following the flow of the waves over the easy ocean floor. Following the whisper of the waves.

There was always foaming water at the bay near the house in Chatham. We shared it with my mother's side of the family. The old house had been built by Justice Brandeis but my mother had never met him, just his daughter, her Aunt Elizabeth, or E. B.

Nick and Anna and I used to swim in the bay, and we learned to sail a Sunfish there and to fish there, though once a fishhook went clean through my lip and I had to walk up to the house without fainting to show my mother and Joe. Once I'd seen the look in my mother's eye, though, I did faint.

When I woke up from surgery, I went down to the beach house and examined all my fishing tackle. Realizing: I'd picked it all out myself, the most demonstratively sharp, monstrous, and deadly-looking hooks you could imagine. Having considered at the time, obviously, that the sharper the hook, the harder it was to pull back though the fish. But having now had the experience of being hooked, it made me sad that I had been so unconsciously and unthinkingly sadistic, and I poured all my hooks into a hole in the ground.

After Joe carried me off to bed that night and I had buried myself under the stiff, old summer house sheets and starchy wool blankets, I saw the ghost of Aunt E. B.

I'd always found elderly women frightening, especially since that episode of *The Brady Bunch* where they went to Hawaii and met Vincent Price in a cave and he'd told them the legend of the Shark Queen. But E. B. seemed nice to me. Nice like the grandmother in a TV movie.

She told me not to worry so much about fish. They

were merely manifestations of the physical realm. If you let yourself care about such small things, you would spend the rest of your life anxious and obsessive.

"You were not born to be a nitpicky little freak, you were born to be strong. Can't you see? Why hell, Quentin, think about my father. Think about Louis Brandeis. All his life they called him a Hebrew and a kike and a hymie and a Jesus killer and a Shylock and a yid and a nickel nose, and all kinds of other things. But he took it all in turn and never raised a fist.

"When I was little, he'd say to me, 'Elizabeth, success is the best revenge.' And of course he went on to become a Supreme Court Justice and has a university named after him. You would do well to remember that, Quentin. You can think like a *fish* all you want to, but you must always be a *man* if you want the waves to take you landward."

At the end of every summer on Cape Cod, with dread in our hearts, we'd return home to the city for school. Waiting as late as we could, we'd get all our back-to-school crap at Ames or Woolworth's and move loose-lidded and sloppy-limbed home through nightmare end-of-summer traffic, with songs like "Baker Street" and "Boys of Summer" playing somewhere while the weight of the humid night crushed itself against us.

My mother had a sweet habit of asking Nick and Anna and me to say goodbye to places and things. We'd always say goodbye to the Brandeis house and the little pump house. And goodbye to the fish in the sea and the geese just leaving and the loons just landing. Goodbye to the crickets in the soft grass and the worms burrowing in the dirt underneath.

But I didn't want to leave.

And I'd think: Bury me there, I'll be fine, really I will, you won't miss me at all, I'll just skip school this year. Find me up here next summer with my new friends Bluejay and Bear, Owl, and Bunny. We've made quite a little bungalow for boys and beasts in the old pump house.

No ghosts here, mom. No ghosts here E.B. and Justice Brandeis. Say hello to Frog and Badger. Say hello to my new friends. But never.

Never.

Never say goodbye.

*****

In Stuyvesant Town the old people lingered with boot and tongue and chastised us children for riding our BMX bikes where we did. My thick blond hair had grown scraggy and Yas had a small inky Afro, and we planned on becoming professional BMX riders. There was a film on cable we'd taped onto VHS called *Rad,* and it was our copybook, our playbook, our future-shaped template.

In and out of the sloping brick buildings, I tended to prefer *out:* away from stepmother and the incessant fighting and the futile mind games she and I played.

I had trained myself not to look directly into the winking black holes of her eyes, but if I did accidentally, she'd scream "What are you staring at?" and push me aside, green carpet underfoot, as she made her way to the fridge for a Tab.

She'd turn to me and say, "Do you remember that time you wouldn't eat the watermelon I gave you but when your dad came back then you had some? Did you think it was poisoned?"

And I'd pretend and say, "I can't remember."

And she'd flicker with slanted laughter: "Oh fuck you! I know you're lying. You got a memory like an elephant."

In the darkness of our Stuyvesant Town palace I can remember Yas telling on me for something and Jocelyn running into the room to beat me, my supine boy's form on the bunk bed with sheets on it advertising Disney's *The Black Hole.*

Smoke voices fighting in the night and the sounds of blows and things breaking. A look to Yas: I can't hear it if you can't. You are my friend and I will always try to love you, here with our treasure of bikes and toys, even if it is *her* blood that runs through the cold sea of your veins.

And we could smile and we could hug, joylessly, because even if we had each other, it still wasn't enough protection. Even little boys, proud and boastful, must sometimes fight in wars against adults with elbows like lances and the jousting sick of fists to their slushy still-growing stomachs.

One day I said to Yas, "Let's ride bikes!"

And he shook his head broadly, like a bull with horns, and said, "I don't feel like it."

"How come?"

"I don't ever wanna ride bikes again."

"Why not?"

"Because we're never gonna be any good. We're never gonna become pros. It's a waste of time, and it's stupid."

His dark eyes rustled at me.

I said, "All the pros say they didn't set out to become pros, they just did it 'cause it was fun. We have fun, don't we?"

"You're just saying that because it's what the pros say.

We don't always have fun. We try real hard and mess up a lot and it sucks. And you're way worse than me."

"I know."

"You're never gonna be a pro."

"I know. But it's fun."

"You're just convincing yourself it's fun 'cause the pros say it's supposed to be fun. But you wouldn't be doing it if someone told you you'd never be pro."

Silence on my end. Halted breathing.

"You know what you are, Quentin?"

"No."

"You're a poser."

"Nuh unh."

"Yeah, you are. You're a poser. You just like having a cool bike and cool gear and cool clothes but you suck at doing tricks and you fall all the time."

He turned away, back to his Nintendo or his comic book, and I sat there looking at his back as winter whistled bright and windy outside our window glass. When I looked at my reflection in a dark triangle it was too big, magnified, and made me look like a ten-foot tall imbecile.

*****

A few weeks later, I punched my fist through a different window. I remember feeling frustrated and testing the strength of the glass with my fingers. The next thing I knew, my arm was halfway through it and bleeding. I was only in my underwear and I rolled down the stairs and onto the cold wood floor wailing, "Kill me! Kill me!"

"Kill me!" I cried, huddled into a naked bloodball of flesh on the cold wood floor as my mother tried to pry me open to see where the wound lay.

I had just missed the vein on my forearm in two spots, but the cuts were deep enough to leave lasting scars that are awfully hard to explain except to say, "When I was a boy, I put my fist through a window."

*****

That same year I flew over the eyeballs of the ocean to England with my mother's family, and when I woke rays of cloud entered my window and whispered the *Benny Hill* theme song in my ear. We stayed near Russell Square at the Penn Club, a Quaker establishment for travelers, where we drank tea and peered around doorways and ate runny eggs. Quakers with wrinkled faces and quick fingers flitted unsteadily around the place and looked at us with wondering eyes.

"We are from America," I would tell them.

"Of course you are, boy."

And I would smile, unashamed, and ask, "Is this a shilling or a pence?"

In the gray holdfast of our room, Nick taught me to play Dungeons and Dragons. We went on an adventure together down the road to look for hamburgers but could only find "beefburgers" at a place called Wimpy's. Nick tried to order a vanilla milkshake but the woman kept repeating his word as "banilla," and when it arrived it was banana. Nick took a sip and gave me a leer that made me almost pee in my pants.

Leaving London, the roads bent south and north and the green lines and well-shaped hills moved me in the way only novelty can move a child. We stayed at bed and breakfasts with tinderboxes and fried tomatoes; one of them was owned by the singer from Duran Duran's parents. Nick and Anna and I, who did not always get along, formed a sort of team that month. We were child crusaders prepared to bring all that was good in American culture to the English.

In the form of sustained metaphor we actually got lost in a quick-mocking fog on the moors, trampling purple heather underfoot and calling out to one another.

In Dorset, at the green, burnt skeleton of Corfe Castle, I grew obsessed with climbing a certain wall. Its stone had the look of millions of whelks and shells like leopard spots, and it was easy to climb. Handy spots to put a foot over. Without really thinking about what I was doing, I just kept ascending, digging a thumb in here, a toe in there. Proudly rising above all the tourists and the occasional spikes and spears of my own family. The air blew oddly in my face as I reached the summit, oldly in my face as I took in all of England, all around me, the arms of old England in all-important embrace.

And then I realized how high I was, got vertigo, and began to cry.

"Help!"

Thirty or so feet below I could see gray-headed folk in anoraks and hiking shoes, looking around for the source of the call and finally pointing upwards. *There he is! The mad child! He's gone and clambered up the rock face, he has! Where's his parents?* And then they too arrived and pointed up to me in the English afternoon, misty and green with a hint of madness.

"Quentin! Get down from there right now!"

"I can't."

"What?"

"I get dizzy when I look down."

"What did he say? Oh for crying out loud!"

"Right mad that one is, the little imp. Climbing up all that ways himself."

A crowd had formed below me, human-shaped with invisible faces, and I could see Nick conferring with my mother and Joe shaking his head and then finally a wiry bearded man beginning to climb the wall. His boots found easy footholds as sand and pebbles rubbed off and fell beneath them, and his hands dug into the flats and crooks of chalk and stone as he rose.

Quick and easy he made it to the top, and smiled at me.

"Well there, lad, you enjoying yourself?"

I laughed a little through my tears.

"Persistent little bugger, aren't you?"

"I just . . . I didn't see how high I was getting."

"Your eyes were bigger than your stomach, eh?"

"I guess."

"Alright, come here then. That's right. Piggyback-like. Hold on."

And so I descended the wall, hugging tightly to this man's back. His hair was shiny and smelled of tobacco and wool, like an afternoon of cigarettes in some taverny attic room. The wind blew in our faces, our ruddy cheeks, wild wind and sea wet on our cheeks, and I began to dread the scolding to come, so clung tighter to the stranger as he stepped off the last of the stones.

"There we are."

What came next was an abstruseness of How Could You's and Why Would You's, but I had no answers. What could I say? *It seemed like a good idea at the time.* I wasn't trying to get away from you all so much as get a better viewpoint, perspective. To see the world around us in its full flow and not be caught down there in that green scene. I am sorry.

That night, getting ready for bed, with the whispering sounds of cows regardant over the moon-mastered land, Nick turned to me and said, "You really are crazy, you know that?"

"Yeah, I guess."

"That shit you pulled with the window, when you broke that window."

"Yeah."

"That really fucked up my summer plans."

"Huh?"

"I was gonna go to Montreal with Matt and Scott, and then your mom said I had to stay."

"How come?"

"In case you tried to pull any other crazy shit."

"I don't get it."

"We had you on suicide watch, you idiot."

"But I broke it by mistake. I wasn't gonna jump out."

"Yeah right."

"For real."

"What about today, then?"

"It was a mistake."

"Yeah right."

"It was."

"Fuck that. You climbed up there 'cause you were gonna jump, and then you chickened out just like last time."

"No way. I don't want to die."

"Sure you don't."

"But it's true."

"You just think you don't wanna die, but part of you really does and you can't see it."

"Huh."

As I lay down in my hard bed with its sheets that smelled of mutton and orange Tang, I tried to wrap my mind around what Nick had said. I couldn't close my eyes, only narrow them, and as the night weakened, they felt like stones, white stones with lids too small and lids too rough, and it kept hitting me in the face, this notion, like the bristles of kitten's whiskers licking: duality.

Two poles of awareness existing in one brain.

******

Yas turned into a man while I was away in England. He'd discovered *Appetite for Destruction* and made it to third base. Now he wore his shirts open to reveal a bare chest and had a girlfriend called Layla down the road from our summer rental in Woodstock.

Layla and her best friend Stormy were both fourteen. Stormy and I would watch MTV together while Yas and Layla made out on the sofa nearby. Hand-jobs, fingering, you name it. I had three more years before my voice would break and just wanted to be home reading comic books or playing Mario Bros. But here I was with a couple of future porn stars, drinking light beer and trying to smoke cigarettes without coughing.

Stormy was blond with a face out of Hogarth. She was a woman and I was some kind of mollusk who could only sit there spinelessly. Was growing old really all about beer, cigarettes, handjobs, and the golden tonsils of Axl Rose?

Stormy and Layla and later, their male friend Dylan, seemed to not have parents. To have been abandoned at some point. Dylan owned a crossbow and let me fire it once, though not before he'd aimed it at me several times.

Once he said something very odd to me.

He said, "I wish I could line up twenty virgin hookers behind a fence and have sex with each of them through a hole in it."

I WISH I COULD LINE UP TWENTY
VIRGIN HOOKERS BEHIND A FENCE

CHAPTER THREE

(Kools, "Stuck in the Middle with You," yellow roses, Sarah's sock drawer, and first fondue)

My father bought a terraced house on a clotted hill of houses named after a salad. My stepmother had never learned to swim, stalled upon her city girl throne, but insisted on a house with an indoor pool. Once we moved she barricaded herself inside and started ordering doll collections and deep fat fryers and miniature cars off the QVC channel like mad.

The bottom of the house, where the pool lay, had been a dentist's office. This became Yasunari's room and mine, to share. Nothing was done to redecorate; I believe there was even a dentist's chair left. Bright fluorescents overhead mastered our eyes and the constant brume of chlorine in the air made them red and our noses run.

Eventually the pool grew stagnant and swamp-green and, after a serpentine battle of chemicals and germs, it was emptied and became a place for skateboarding and band practice.

Years before that happened, Yas made his first friend in town. His name was Gary and he looked just like Vanilla

Ice. He drove a white sedan with tinted windows around town with his subwoofers blasting this rap song – you could only hear the bass and kick drum – that went *Ba Da Ba Da* pause *Ba Da Ba Da* pause. Years later, Tool's song "Sober" used the same beat.

Gary was a junior in high school and Yas and I were thirteen when they started hanging out. And while Yas was a mature thirteen, I was not. I'd beg off having to hang out with Gary, but they'd both call me pussy until I went along. And there *was* a certain razorlike thrill to coasting around night-worn suburbs in Gary's car with nothing to do but always the promise of some fantastic event around the corner.

These events usually proved to be keg parties at The Eagle or Rockwood, which were a statue of an eagle near some train tracks and a plot of grass by a hospital respectively. Somehow, in the lingua franca of Tarrytown teenage worthies, these places had been certified gold as cop-free hangout zones. But before hitting The Eagle or Rockwood came the endless quest for beer. Yas and I both had fake IDs, though mine said I was younger than I actually was. I'd acquired it, to the soundtrack of much mockery, to get into movies at children's rates. Yas's ID said he was twenty-one and went to NYU and it sometimes worked. But mostly we found ourselves at the mercy of the Hispanic population of North Tarrytown, who everyone called *yanyos*. So Gary and Yas taught themselves to say *me compre cerveza*, and that was our lifeline to the Coronas.

Deep in the night-green matins of Rockwood, we'd find football players and cheerleaders and an assortment of sanguine teenage beer drinkers. Some wore bandanas. Some played Grateful Dead songs on their guitars. And some might yell out a request for "Wish You Were Here." Others wore penny loafers with white socks and rugby shirts. The young women had tapered jeans and ribbed sweaters with turtlenecks popping out from underneath, and their hair was curly on purpose and greasy with product.

Yas had grown short dreadlocks and was called Milli by the denizens of this loveless new world, which made me Vanilli, being the lighter-skinned one.

These were high school juniors and seniors, creeping nightward to the world of college with beer and sex alone to play peekaboo with. To watch the hobbling jerkined dance of teenage mating rituals prematurely, with no notion of the sensations involved, was not so different from watching my babysitter masturbate: I could see how important it all was to them, but I couldn't for the life of me understand why.

And then someone handed me a joint.

******

Before marijuana, high school was a hive of deep deprivation for me. Trying out new looks, riding my bike aimlessly around Brooklyn, and reading D.H. Lawrence's poem "Ship of Death" over and over. I read Dostoyevsky for extra credit. I was impressed by the clockwork unraveling — or raveling. I should say — of Raskolnikov's guilt under Porfiry's scrutiny.

Twenty-one years later, when I published a spy novel consisting entirely of plagiarized passages, I would go through a similar set of experiences. But *Crime and Punishment* would be far from my thoughts.

Meanwhile my hair had gone from blond to brown and my voice had finally changed, but, as if in compensation, my eyes went bad. I chose not to wear glasses so I wouldn't have to see the world too clearly and hoped people saw me the same way.

Cannabis carried me from being a timid kid into a summer world of teenaged punks and alternateens at the Bennington July Program. Possession of the substance – and the ability to smoke it with objects as mundane as an apple or soda can – brought friends and admirers.

My best friend there was a handsome boy with dark eyes named Stewart, who'd go on to enjoy a very brief career as a rock star in the band Jonathan Fire*Eater. Stewart and I had a band that July with a counselor named Jason, and played covers of VU, Galaxie 500, and Neil Young.

We got to be quite the men about town. Besides the July Program, Bennington had a concurrent series of writing workshops for adults. There were readings every night up the hill from us at the Deane Carriage Barn. For some reason we were the only two students to avail ourselves of this and were soon hobnobbing and drinking wine with poets like Gerald Stern, Linda Gregg, and Sharon Olds a few nights a week.

When our counselor and bandmate Jason found out, he joined us, and it was on one of these occasions that we convinced the organizers of the reading series to let us play. When this finally did happen, we were all so nervous we got way too high beforehand and opened with an eight-minute version of "Down by the River." To this day, one of my favorite all-time memories is of seeing W. D. Snodgrass, who had read before we played, sort of dancing and twirling around to our stoned meanderings.

Having found a niche of like-minded young adults that summer made it hard to go back to the jock haven of high school, where white kids, the children of Gramercy Park, talked like black kids and tromped about in a kind of aggressive hormonal confusion.

Where once I was good to them for letting them cheat off me and borrow my homework, now I was of interest as a smoker and procurer of controlled substances. Snoop Dogg and Dr. Dre's *The Chronic* had hit, and 40s of Olde English, ganja smoke, and emptied-out cigar casings were the flavor of the season.

I played the electric bass in our school jazz band, but that didn't help. I wrote poetry late into the night, and that certainly didn't help. Uninterested in any subject but English, my mind developed on its own like a flailing tree in quarantine. I tried looking to Lawrence, Miller, and Céline for some insight into this condition.

I'd suffered from hideous acne the year before and used a kind of medical paste that quite literally burned the blemishes from my skin. At sixteen, my face was red and raw like a baby's. The redness bothered me so much, gave me such a sense of being exposed, that I experimented briefly with make up. It was a freakish thing to do in those days, long before emo and too too long after glam or even Robert Smith, and I was quickly and thoroughly ridiculed out of it.

Late on Christmas Eve of that year I was chased by a car full of Puerto Rican men through the abandoned streets of Park Slope. I was in good shape and made it about six blocks down Prospect Park West before they caught me. They took my watch and my winter coat, broke my glasses, and tried to beat me up. Four against one is tough odds, but I made it out with only one black eye and a deviated septum.

I remember the hard wind against my face and the hope that an old restaurant called Rain Trees would be open, the turn onto Ninth Street, the hard fear, and the hope of outracing a motorcar.

*****

In 1992, my musical tastes met with Yasunari's at the unlikely, unsteady, and ungirdled node of "alternative rock." Suddenly with the Lemonheads and Buffalo Tom and Dinosaur Jr. and Sonic Youth and Pavement and Superchunk and all else that was great that year, we agreed on something aesthetically. In that wintertime and into that bleak then soft spring, we were making mixtapes, reading zines, wearing striped T-shirts and cords and Chuck Taylors, and even trying to write our own songs.

Then one day we got tickets to see Dinosaur Jr. play at the Ritz. The band that opened for them were pale and gray in their attitude and attire and took ages to set up their endless Marshall stacks. When they were finally ready, they walked out on stage, two men and two women, and without smiling, without really looking at anything, they picked up their instruments and counted in to the loudest and most beautiful song I'd ever heard.

It was called "Only Shallow" and the band was My Bloody Valentine. The volume they played at alone fluttered and winged adrenaline through my insides, and my eardrums flamed up with silver sweet bird calls. It was the sound of the future, a certain future; it picked me up out of what was familiar, and dropped me somewhere new, where the slow bells of memory merged with the blended voices of childhood suicide songs.

Years later, in college, it would turn out that at least four of my best friends were at that same show at the Ritz when the band played one note from "You Made Me Realize" for forty minutes straight. But as a wee lad of fifteen, never having heard *Isn't Anything* or *Ecstasy and Wine,* or conceived of the notion of playing a detuned guitar with the tremolo bar on every chord, I merely thought I was hearing music made by creatures from some other, finer dimension. The hoot and roar of elephants stomping through a prismatic melody stream.

*****

The winter after Bennington I visited Stewart in D.C. He picked me up at Union Station and we got high, went for pizza, and ran into some dudes who sold us some acid. Stewart and me and a few kids we knew didn't wear baggy clothes at this time when it was *de rigueur.* We wore corduroy jeans and Rockfords or New Balance with striped sweaters and gas station jackets. It was interesting, watching Stew complete the transaction with these baggy jeans types.

The next night we took the LSD. I remember we went to Adams Morgan, to a bar called Hell. Later we caught a ride in a pick-up truck to sisters Leni and Diana's house, where I studied the coffee-table works of Hieronymus Bosch for hours. Or maybe minutes. Stew had been drinking, wisely I realized, and had passed out back home. I was up all night in his dermatologist father's study, looking at encyclopedias of rare skin diseases.

When I got back to school I made some subtle inquiries into who sold the acid. When finally procured, the paper tabs had little McDonald's Ms on them. The McDonald's tabs were the strongest and the purest acid I ever took. Wandering through the streets of Tarrytown after abandoning an uneaten meal at T. G.I. Friday's, a series of parking garages became a Greco-Roman coliseum full of columns and antechambers and withheld truths. Asking my friend Jacqueline for a pen and paper, I'd write down something like, "There are ten thousand layers to this thing called Man." But mostly we just laughed as our spinal fluid rushed overdrive to our pleasure receptors.

Though aware of the dangers, I began to use LSD as a kind of recreational drug though my junior year of high school. I slunk about the corridors of the old orange and brown bunker with an intermingled sense of shame and pride, until one day in the spring I smoked some hash and the high lasted for six or seven days. Seven days of DNA-strand rollercoasters twisting like vines around anything I looked at, and panic attack-type chest constriction.

Death, I was sure, was around any corner, so I wrote a love poem for my squash coach, which she kindly never brought up. I remember one line was: *Deliver me into your blood.*

Squash had been a game that was, at least aesthetically, enjoyable while high: the white clothes, the white courts, how the angle you hit the ball resounded in a spectacular number of possibilities for return, involving both the back and front walls and a series of arbitrary parameters marked off by painted red lines. But the experience of being high for seven days put me off drugs altogether for a very long time, and suddenly squash bored me to tears.

Out of the blue there was this gaping, almost wound-like hole in the knitting of my days, and what did I choose to fill it with?

Jogging.

In some desperate effort to gain control once more, I grabbed the reins, studied for the SATs, learned that alien language, and started jogging a few miles every day. I'd gained twenty pounds in my laissez-faire days, and I decided I must be fat. The truth is, I was approaching six feet and weighed 160 pounds. I preferred to be about 140. The problem was, no one else preferred that.

So I spent the summer of 1993 running up to thirteen miles a day and working in Central Park with a bunch of very well-meaning Jamaicans who thought I'd landed from Mars. No one could pronounce my last name as anything but "Ron," so I became Ron to all and sundry for the rest of the summer while I cleaned the fountain on Fifty-Ninth Street and planted shrubs around Sheep's Meadow. Every day we'd watch the digital clock on the old bank building, and if the temperature went above 96 degrees we could drop everything and leave.

That was the green time. Leaves fluting around head and feet, and old cobblestones caterpillaring through tea-time tunnels to rise out into lava-like mounds of granite and duck ponds. The lunchtime crowd sweltering with soft American sandwiches, and besunglassed Asians lolling on the green benches like overheated midget St. Bernards before the evening time. When I'd wake up from a nap in the late afternoon, with the universal motor hum of the city just dying, there was nowhere to go.

Home, where my mother would tell me I was getting too skinny or home, where my father was proud I could run thirteen miles.

That was the green time, before the evening time, or wrapped up inside it like sweaty August lovers spooning, the red letters of the old New Yorker building, and beyond them the purple sky wastes of Hoboken, New Jersey. Clip clop through the night wood park, to the north and to the west where streams ran through Olmsted's blackened hills and men went to have anonymous sex. Clop clip further down and east to the world of Fifth Avenue and expensive psychotherapists who smiled but didn't say much. Clip clop through the nighttime meadow at 79th, where the drug dealers still remembered me so why didn't I stop when they waved? Old theaters like the Paris showing movies from Eastern European countries where naked women talked philosophy to men with big noses, or further down to Fifth and Fifty-Seventh to the artificial waterfall I liked to stare at when I was tripping.

This was the green time. Nowhere to go but underground where it was hotter. Or run over the bridge. 13-mile-a-day man. Green time. *Feelin' dirty*. Over the bridge. *And gritty*. To the firefly lights of a million officemen who forgot to turn off the lights in their million officemen boxes. To the rising coils of cables suspending me and other tons of things above the naked cheek of the water. The blue embrace. In the green time. Where the sandhogs had died and the Roebling family prospered in those cosmopolitan days of German opera and Lenape riverboat casinos.

******

When I got back to school senior year, they said, "You look so skinny you must have AIDS or be shooting up."

"But I've just been running a lot, I swear."

"Well, put twenty pounds on, will you, or you can't come back to school. And we're going to need you to take some tests."

Or: "You look good."

Or: "You look terrible, man."

Or: "You look like perhaps you're just a filter for people's personal notions on aesthetics and things."

And finally: "Back to the old games, yeah?"

The old pursuits. Getting good grades? Gah. Editing the lit mag? Gah. Applying to colleges? Gah.

But it had to be done.

Once I'd been accepted to the college with the picture of the planet earth on its brochure, I picked up a beer. I did, I did. Maybe even a pitcher.

"I stand corrected."

It was senior year at one of those old pizza joints with pitcher beer in the West Village that didn't card – well, no one did until 1994 – and I was with Yas and his German girl.

"Was it exhilarating?"

Not that I hadn't been drunk before, but this time, after months and months of control both physical and mental, to allow that part of my brain to shut off for a minute.

"To not worry, jeez."

That felt good. People laughed at my jokes and told me I was weird and even if we were just sitting inside our petty little mind-bubble of drunkenness, it felt lovely.

"Why hadn't you done this more?"

Clearly it was a secret the world had been keeping from me. Too much of a good thing, etc, Well, fuck that, I said. I said, "I'm going to get drunk all the time from now on."

And I did.

So somehow this half-English skinny girl from school came aboard and we started making out and I felt so mature, but then I could never really remember it. And the elusiveness of that made me want to do it again, but the fear of doing it without alcohol, well, you get it.

"A cycle begins to form."

Memory me a dark bedroom. She put on that record *The Cross of Changes* by Enigma, and we started cracking up. Her breasts were tiny blackberries, and I treated them with great respect.

HIS THIRD EYE IS BUSTED

CHAPTER FOUR

(take a whiff, pull it out, the taste is gonna move you when you pop it in your . . . pop it in your . . .)

There were three of us: Bluesman Paul, Bluesman Paul's friend, and me. We drank some vodka that was only there for display and replaced it with water. We watched part of a really decrepit porno from the seventies and got into a wrestling match. Maybe I didn't know my own strength or maybe vodka brought out some long-dormant Hulk inside me, but I threw BP's friend against the glass mirror and the whole thing shattered around him. Uncut, unfazed, I still assumed he'd be pissed, but he just started laughing.

We all started laughing.

And then BP's mom came in screaming and threw us all out of the house. Well, now hold on there a minute, missy, I thought, and took the vodka bottle with me into the bathtub, where I promptly passed out and turned on the shower nozzle with my head. BP and his friend heard the shower and rushed in to find me lying there, clothed, bottle to my lips with the cold water raining over me.

I must have already had alcohol poisoning because I

was already puking. They gave me a garbage bag to puke into as we left. Apparently we went all over the city that night and had a grand old time, but I can only remember the EMS guys trying to wake me and carting me off the hospital to have my stomach pumped.

Thus begins the chapter about the last year of high school and the first year of college and all the things I can't remember about them.

******

I managed to explain away the hospital incident to my parents as having to do with breaking up with the half-English girl, and they half-believed me and let me go see Stew's band play at Under Acme that evening. I was in pretty rough shape. Stella bought me a beer and I could barely finish it. Stew's band was jarring and not very good. Granted, they would get very good indeed, and soon, and perhaps even better when they became the Walkmen, but in 1993 they were just college freshmen posturing in tight suits and doing a semi-decent impression of Nick Cave backed by the Nation of Ulysses. But it still sounded kind of scary.

So I was a blackout drinker. Not wholly ideal. For it would mean so often, as things progressed, my own story was told back to me like so many other tales. And it never sounded like *me* to me, these reminiscences of wild drunkenness and depravity. They was something very Mr. Hyde-like about it all, these shadow games I'd get up to and rediscover later like a memory detective.

Most important to me was hiding it from my father. The thought of disappointing him was more than I could bear. There was also this notion I had of being a sort of secret agent man. Sneaking the booze in, or out. Acting sober and having serious conversations when I was dead drunk, etc. Because in my case, by seventeen the physical craving was so insistent that I'd find myself drinking alone in my room on a weeknight, just because I had to. But it was still easy then to find some illicit thrill in the notion of secret teenage transgressions.

In the trees outside my window overlooking the back garage of Key Food, I could see the snow was melting and soon the last year of high school would be coming to an end.

I had a brief "affair" with a girl at Yas's high school who played drums in an all-girl band called Raggedy Anne. Yas and I got drunk on 40s on the Metro North train south and went to see her band play at Under Acme. Her parents were there and could clearly tell I was hammered.

Meanwhile, Yas went off to buy weed in Washington Square Park and got arrested. They put him in the paddy wagon with the dealer and the dealer slipped him his beeper through the cuffs and told him, "Call my woman, Jamilla."

I was just about to leave without him when Yas came running around the corner with a summons in one hand and a beeper in the other. We called the number for Jamilla and told her her man was in prison, but she sounded nonplussed.

"Well, what should we do with the beeper?" we asked.

"Keep it, mon."

*****

The drummer girl never called me again. Other "prospects" lurked around the slushy corners of the iceberg horizon, however. I'd made friends with a boy named Rafe who was white but wore a large Afro. We'd get drunk together and get up to some trouble here and there. Just pish and posh.

One night that winter I blacked out and tripped on some ice. I got a pretty bad gash in the middle of my forehead. Leaned up against a wall, apparently I kept saying, "Who am I? Who am I?" over and over.

Rafe told me later someone had commented: "His third eye is busted. He can't see so good."

Rafe was in an outdoors club thing with the prettiest redhead I'd ever seen. On a camping trip she told him she thought I was cute.

I was intimidated enough by her, the one and only Cross, that I didn't ask her out for months. And meanwhile word of my escapades had spread enough that the top kids in our class wanted to get to know me before it was all gone.

Green grass and clover all the world over.

One such person was a very mature girl named Kate who looked like Kelly Lebrock in *Weird Science* with long brown hair and sultry French lips and danced in a cage at a club called the Tunnel on weekends. She invited me to come watch her sometime. It turned out to be the night of our jazz band's big concert, Jazz Night!

Afterwards, Yas and I drank a bottle of red wine each walking west across Manhattan. By the time we got there, I was already in a blackout.

So from hearsay: the doorperson's name was Genitalia and s/he thought we were cute. Yas sat me down on a bench and left me there. Some transvestites tried to take me home with them saying all I needed was "a bath and a blow job." Just as all that was happening Mark Wahlberg (he was still Marky Mark then) walked by, and I projectile-vomited on his sneakers. Perturbed, he stepped toward me. And I apparently shot up from my stupor and challenged him. Kate and my stepbrother had found me by this time and advised me against it.

My one big brush with fame.

*****

I ran into J at a college fair at the old Ethical Culture Society building on Prospect Park West. We'd both switched schools around fifth grade and lost touch. He took a long look at me with his blue eyes and could tell, it seemed, that I had changed, my long swoop of hair and ungraceful vintage clothes perhaps signifying to him the vulnerable drug-dazzle of recent days.

He looked exactly the same, just older. There was a kind of gentle withdrawal to him, somehow more bright and new than my own bright and new that had to do, I finally saw, with the dictates of personality and emotional resolve more than all-important fads or gestures or speech.

"Hey!"

"Hey, wow. Look at you."

"Ha ha."

"You thinking of going here?"

"I think so, yeah. Might apply early decision."

"Wow. Yeah, I'm not sure."

"I just want to get it over with."

"It's a big decision to make in a hurry, though."

"Maybe, yeah."

"I just don't want to rush into anything."

"How's your mother?"

"She's good."

"Still shopping at the Co-op?"

"Of course. Yours?"

"Co-op for life."

"Yeah. Hah."

"Ever talk to anyone? Nate? Adam?"

"Not really, no."

"Yeah, me neither."

In the intervening years we'd lost our rapport somehow. We were looking at the same college in the Midwest but in the end he didn't go. The science program wasn't strong enough. Either way, the lights went out and we all took our seats in the dark-hushed room to watch a slideshow of green lawns and cold towers and happy students smiling into the deep blue day.

In the dark it was okay.

I was running away then, from the waves and nips of childhood, and wanted only not to remember the drone of sadness and its echo. It would be many years before I could look back once more and see J still standing there on high ground, his secret father's son, saying, "Just step outside of time and wanting and the spoils of your obsessions." And it would be many years still before I could realize he was the one true friend I had as a child, the only one who never turned on me or surprised me with anger or tried to spur me into something else.

But when the slideshow was over and the lights came back on, all jagged and white, I didn't see him anywhere.

And I wandered through the still galleries and tunnel-systems of the Ethical Culture building looking for him. He'd probably left in the blue dark of the slideshow and I hadn't had a chance to say goodbye.

*****

When Cross and I finally did become an item, school was almost over and the air had grown warm in the public parks of the city. We couldn't go to her house to make out because her mother required she leave her door open, so we made out on lawns in public parks until we were asked to stop. We'd drink beer out of paper bags and smoke bummed cigarettes, and that's what dating was in those days.

It was both romantic and tragic. I could only connect to her or anyone if I was drinking but then the sentiments were maudlin and overdone. But if I was sober, I was brain dead and mute. To not get too drunk, just enough to be caring and articulate, was the trick, and I was able to pull it off well enough mostly.

That summer was the most indolent time of my life. It never occurred to me to get a job. It was just Cross and beer. She was good friends with the lawyer William Kunstler's daughters, and we went to a 4th of July party with them and some of their friends in a sublet on Avenue A above Sidewalk Cafe.

On the roof, the sky was navy blue with comet streaks and noise everywhere, like we were in Saigon. There was a girl there named Aimee who kept trying to make out with me behind Cross's back and stuck a finger up my butt a couple times. I remember passing out on a futon with Cross in front of me and Aimee behind me, fiddling around back there.

Coming to the next morning was a holocaust of the senses, the heat, the smell, my contact lenses fried to my eyes, and remembering I hadn't called home.

Having once been one for being organized and making imaginary lines in my head around things, I felt I had now fallen off the graph paper entirely. When I was a boy, I used to write out lists of everything I was going to wear that week and what activities I intended to take part in. And here I was, hair long and unkempt, in seventies-era thrift-store clothes, living on grilled cheese sandwiches, drifting about the Village with only beer and Cross on my mind.

Best was our time in Vermont. Together for a week in the country, with no beer, we got on surprisingly well, playing cards on an old bear rug, canoeing, listening to *Siamese Dream* over and over. Sitting in the woods one night, smoking cigarettes with the smoke from the stone chimney sweeping past us and the moon above us like a mongoloid star, I remember wanting to stop time. It's true: maybe the purest experience of young love I ever felt. Before we learned about things like mind games and all that.

So much was to change, and so much was to go wrong before it went right only to go wrong again, but there, that I could always be there with my head on her naked, pale, and sun-freckled belly on that flat-wood bed, in that gingerbread house, in those anonymous woods, miles from any other house and with only the lilt of the spring and the creak of the twig, to-wit to-woo, to lull us to summer sleep.

CHAPTER FIVE

(welcome to the camp, I guess you all know the way to north quad, margarita mix, el duce was his biggest supporter, déjeuner sur Honey Power)

That August, the idle underlip of higher education subsumed me in its terrene loincloth. It was warm still, with the wind blowing red on our faces and all the lawns rolled down toward the green of Wilder Bowl, where the mailroom combined with other services we would need at one time or the other in the next four years. You could get a thing called a crispy patty there. Anxious freshmen filled the rooms of oddly space-age buildings in search of this or that prof who was supposed to be the best, while a species of human hitherto unknown to me, the Voice Major, strutted about in scarves in summer trilling arias from *Tosca*.

Talcott was the voice major dorm; someone should have warned me. My roommate was okay enough, I guess, from Maryland or somewhere and really into jazz piano. He set up his lame keyboards everywhere and was always locking me out so he could have sex with his girlfriend, who had followed him from Maryland or wherever. We didn't last long as roommates because, frankly, I was always drunk and something about that seemed to disturb him.

So classes started and I'd say to myself, "No drinking this week" and "Buckle down," but it solved so many problems in the short term. I remember puzzling over an astounding short story by Henry James about a fellow called Dencombe. I had some ideas about what was going on there, wrote them down, and was promptly told they were wrong. They'd put a sophomore or a junior in the class to head off our papers at the pass, so the professor wouldn't have to lay eyes on the offending articles until they'd been sanitized.

At night I'd talk to Cross on the phone and write her love letters and wander the campus roads with names like Elm and Main and College, down to place called the Arb and past it to your usual cemetery/golf course combo. The quiet of the place was as jarring as all the strange new Midwestern brands of beer.

On one of my aimless rambles to or from the library I ran into a blond girl with rosy skin from Brattle Street named Hillary. We started talking and it turned out she'd gone to Andover and had a boyfriend back home, but they were having troubles. I told her I was in a similar situation and we wound up making out in the grass till very late that night.

*****

There was a certain aesthetic algebra to college life that was extremely pleasing, the notebooks clacking on hardwood desks and pens rustling out of backpacks stuffed with stacks of textbooks with "used" on their spines. At first my fellow students' zeal surprised me, coming as I did from a place where no one really cared much about learning things. Then I began to realize I was tragically far behind for that very reason. Drinking the way I did didn't help. With a shaky wisp of shame, I'd tell myself to straighten out and focus, and that kind of resolve would sometimes get me to the weekend.

I'd considered becoming an anthropology major freshman year and tried to use what I'd learned in class to make prescient observations about the garish young adult empire around me, but certain symbolic rituals kept tripping me up: the Friday night kegger, for instance, with its crackling armada of smolderingly liberal young women all trying to outdo one another in regards to hair color, piercings, and indie-rock credentials. It was at one of these keg parties that I met Jen and Dave and we formed a band.

Jen was half-Swedish with brown hair and had the highest, finest cheekbones and fairy bright eyes I'd ever seen. Dave was from New Jersey and had been in a band called Native Nod. Back then he always wore this Superman hat.

A week or so after our first practice, Jen showed up at my room with a bottle of gin and I cheated on Cross again. Jen, I felt, could teach me things about music and stuff, like what was cool in London, that kind of thing. She had a voice like Kristin Hersh and wrote heartbreaking songs.

That first night we spent together there were always flashing Christmas lights on somewhere, making her milky-soft breasts and translucent flesh alien blues and greens. And afterward I had to run to art class, still drunk, to paint naked men for three hours.

At Thanksgiving break I broke up with Cross. I remember getting into a fight with my mother because I didn't want to wear a gray wool suit and then a distant relative, old Hugh, asking me if I was old enough for the hard stuff, to which I replied, yes, I absolutely was.

All in all, pretty dissolute. Trying to push Cross out of my mind. Going to some Tom Cruise vampire extravaganza. Consumption. Money. Food. Bloodsuckers.

After Thanksgiving, Jen turned me on to Ecstasy. I spent some hours hugging a speaker and taking giant steps around the room.

My only memories are of strobing Christmas lights and darkened rooms where the fluorescence made me almost faint, with occasional runs for food. The fourth song on that Slint record. Seefeel. *Mars Audiac Quintet*. Labradford. Red House Painters. *Carnival of Light*.

And once in a while, when no one was looking, I'd put on "Dig a Pony."

*****

I kept missing classes and losing roommates and gaining roommates and getting mediocre grades and not caring, and so on and so forth. Jen broke up with me in the spring; she'd fallen for my new roommate, Luke, a born-again Christian stoner from Palo Alto, and I went home for spring break and died. I tried calling Cross, which was not welcome by any means, and then I got drunk alone in the kitchen of my mother's house on Pernod and vermouth and whatever odd, sick cooking liqueurs were around. I smelled up the house and was confronted the next morning.

She said, "You should talk to your father about AA meetings." And I said, "I know a guy at school who goes to them. I'll talk to him."

But I got drunk at the airport and spent the rest of the week on a bender, sleeping with a girl called Blossom who was sort of the queen of the hippies and screamed, really screamed when she came. At the end of the week she left me for a hirsute character who went by the moniker "Dirty Ray."

I went to my first AA meeting with the older boyfriend of a girl named Hannah from my vegetarian eating co-op. His name was Big Al and he played the cello. He was tall and Aryan and told me his story before the meeting and I could relate it to it but felt really depressed talking about this stuff in the open. He seemed used to it, and the people at the meeting certainly were, but I'd never been in a situation before where people talked so openly and honestly about their feelings.

I can't remember who spoke or what they said, but I remember I didn't want to drink afterwards and that was revolutionary. It didn't last long though, so if I went to a meeting every day I was cool but if I skipped some – well, I drank a bunch of times that spring. At a champagne formal chasing a girl named Angel, getting overwhelmed by the picture of a can of Budweiser in my economics textbook (inelastic demand), you name it.

But if I went to a meeting the craving went away.

And in the meantime, the semester was over.

My stepsister Anna had done all right working on Nantucket the previous summer, and she recommended it. So that's what I did. With Jen now dating my old roommate, Dave a closer friend, and Big Al my big brother in AA, I got on a bus to New Bedford, where Ishmael met Queequeg and heard the fire sermon before setting sail. I went looking around for the hotel they must have stayed in, but it was now a combination KFC/Taco Bell.

******

The ferry dropped me off on the island at night and the cab ride through town was Paul Revere-esque. I spent two weeks at a youth hostel along the beach, nightswimming with some performance artists and slam poets, and then got a job working for a big hotel that gave me an apartment in town. My roommate's name was Coleman, like the coolers, and he was always trying to get me to listen to and appreciate the artistry of a fellow named Dave Matthews. I was employed to work in the laundry for this big hotel and to drive a truck around the island picking up linens and towels from its private cabanas.

My partner in this endeavor was a Mississippian named Davie. We didn't understand each other very well. His accent was so heavy I couldn't make out a word he said, and I, no doubt, sounded faggy and proper.

As we drove around the cobblestoned streets, rife with history, past the old Quaker graveyard where the bones of my ancestors lay, Davie and I developed a kind of lingua franca. He'd point to a woman and ask me, "You hit that?"

Sometimes I'd say sure. Sometimes I'd ignore him. Sometimes I'd roll my eyes as if to say, "Come on, Davie, enough with this game."

But it was our only game. As the days went by my fear of joining him on the laundry truck increased exponentially. He started playing a techno/house music cassette with one beat over and over and refrains like, "Kick that bitch in the neck!"

Finally, one July morning he asked me "Hit that?" about a woman well into her fifties. When I remarked that she was, perhaps, a bit on the old side for me, he responded, "It don't matter! It's all the same down there!"

I promptly told Davie that I was done with our little Hit That game. He responded that he was going to tell Jay, our gay co-worker at the laundry, that I was a "sister."

Davie did just that when we returned. Jay came running out through the aisles of roiling sweat machines to greet me.

Hollering, "I knew it! I knew it!" To which all the old biddies who folded towels, like Cigarette-Time Ruth and Davie's own mother, Bonita, agreed.

"We knew it all along! Quentin is a sister!"

Later that week Jay invited me to P-town for the weekend.

*****

A couple of Irish girls and a bicycle were to preoccupy me on and off for the rest of the summer. Our employer shipped in all these Irish kids to work under the table and they were really the only people I socialized with, other than Coleman and his endless Dave Matthews tapes. But they weren't the best company for someone trying to stay sober. So mostly I rode my cheap bicycle around to all the different beaches on the island, and went bodysurfing and ate cheap vegetarian sandwiches with too much carrot in them.

Occasionally I'd bike by the old Quaker meeting house and wince with the knowledge I was abandoning my heritage or go by the old whaling museum and think, I should really read all of Melville.

But then something would bring me stupidly back to the present, be it "The Piña Colada Song" or a foghorn trolling over the low town like an ancient albatross in search of her lost sleepytime rhyme.

*****

Sophomore year of college I didn't drink at all. I moved into the hippie dorm by accident and the smell of soy milk and baking bread wafted up to me every morning, intermingled with patchouli and low-grade reefer. There was an already married couple down the hall who introduced themselves to me by saying they bred doves in their room.

I slept with some women that first semester, including a wonderful nymphomaniac poet who'd grown up in a pet store and an incredibly talented Korean installation artist, but I was still hung up on Jen.

I continued to play in the band with Jen and Dave, and in another band called Theta-Ro Maps Club with Dave and Justin (also from Native Nod) and another guy called Jon from Rye Coalition. That first semester flew by like a garbage can in a tornado.

When I came home for Christmas break, there was this letter waiting for me. It was from a guy named David Lehman who edited the *Best American Poetry* series, saying that Adrienne Rich had picked a poem I'd written to be in that year's anthology.

Now the story of that poem is that I wrote it during the psychedelic days at age sixteen, in about thirty minutes in a classroom at the Eugene Lang Center for whatever and whatever. Disguised as a poetry workshop for teens, with a bunch of dudes and ladies whose names you'd see in the *New Yorker*, the whole thing was really a big ad for the Eugene Lang whatever center. The only reason I bring it up is because I wrote the thing in half an hour, I read it to the class, and the teacher simply asked me if I knew what the word "avatar" meant. Notably, the keynote speaker for this shindig said something I'll never forget: "Good writers borrow, great writers steal."

So, back into the Tardis: here it is, 1995, and I'm going to be in this anthology. I hadn't written a word that wasn't part of a paper in over a year and really only cared about music at this point, then suddenly it was like this decision had been made for me. Or not. Some people are probably good at making their own decisions, me not so much. I usually let other people or turns of events dictate. And here was some kind of major signpost, I decided, telling me what my future would be. I am not denying agency in any way. Just saying that I was in a state where it was easier for me to let someone else point out a direction for me. Convenient really, in that I didn't have to think too hard on it.

Back at school in February, my advisor got me into an advanced poetry writing seminar where we'd read one poet a week and then write imitations of them. Lowell, Bishop, Jarrell, Ashbery, Plath, etc. It was neat to be in a class with kids who cared so much about poetry, but mostly I just felt like I was playing catch-up all the time. Like I ought to be be better then I was as a poet to fit into this highly advanced situation. One thing I noticed: everyone else in the class was female. And they already had their special poetry reading accents figured out.

I met a girl who looked like a Siberian warrior priestess. Her name was Pelin and it turned out she was Turkish. She won the big poetry fellowship prize the school gave out each year, and I was runner-up. Her old room was wooden but rusty and box-shaped in an old house that was box-shaped on a street that was part of an unkempt grassy grid on an architectural model. Her hair was dark and long and her skin was porcelain tough and fine. We made love on her floor and read the incomprehensible poems of Turkish people she liked.

In my own reality, I was fumbling with notions of what I actually cared about aesthetically. I knew in fiction I preferred folks like Faulkner and James, who wrote smokescreen prose, scrimwork, hazy-filter stuff that took you this way and that and didn't always cough up a meaning or a truth for you, like an oyster from the mouth of a babe in swaddling clothes. With poetry it was another story; clearly I didn't know enough yet. I loved Merwin. Ashbery appealed but he had no music to him, Tate appealed but he was too goofy in the long run. They both did honestly magic things with words, say in "The Lost Pilot" or "The Tennis Court Oath," but lacked a certain sexiness. I don't mean anything blatant, I refer simply to the idea of reading as a sort of seduction ,with folks like Faulkner and James (in the later novels), and Joyce (in *Dubliners*) really knowing how to put on a good striptease. Not from day-drab nothingness to full-on intercourse, but from cloudiness and want of meaning to sudden insight. Emotional though, huh, always emotional.

So Pelin and I ate olives and bread and drank coffee and water and suddenly the year was over. Me, Dave, Jen, Hilary, Justin, and Dave's girlfriend Toponia had all decided to go to Berkeley for the summer and take extension classes, and at the last minute Pelin decided to go too.

*****

Back in Brooklyn for a few weeks, I furiously scribbled poems. In a matter of six months, my style had gone from utter teenage nakedness to a kind of semi-baroque faux W.S. Merwin. I'd grown obsessed with having some other poems out there – *placed*, as they used to say – when the anthology came out in September. Jay Parisi at *Poetry* was kind and suggested shortening the poems. *Fine Madness* took some. A place called *Urbanus* took one. *Witness* took one. But the poems were all flailingly different from each other. Could have been the work of three different people. Makes sense I guess, I was trying to find a "voice," as they tell you you should in workshops and so on. But wouldn't my voice be the first thing that spills out of my head, clumsy and retching and wicked, or else diamondbright and wondrous, either/or? Is this issue of finding a "voice" as it's taught in Creative Writing classes around this country really a matter of cozying up to several "voices" you like and trying to find your own somewhere right in between them? It makes sense. When

I worked in publishing in the late nineties everything was point C in a comparison.

"It's like Robert Coover meets *Bridget Jones's Diary.*"

"It's *On the Road* as written by Douglas Coupland from his couch."

Pitches.

Pitching is something we talk about in relation to sound, singing voices, timbre, etc. So it makes sense. To find your voice, young wayward soul, you must pitch it, like those Tibetan throat singers, to fall between two points, A and B. Let's say Flann O'Brien and Tom Clancy. Or John Barth and Sapphire. Either way, you're still pitching. And you're pitching somewhere in the modest midwest, hours and light years of sophistication (plus or minus) from what anyone cares about in New York.

Safest to be small, they taught us.

Small, light, self-contained.

CHAPTER SIX

(funky cole redeemer, our family is a Cutco family, Jade baby Jade, sweat smelled like springwater, a cabin in the mountains, into the maelstrom yep yep)

Flew into Berkeley on BOAC and didn't get to bed till the following eventide. Justin and I flew together and found Pelin waiting for us at our new address on Alcatraz Avenue. We had nothing with us but some clothes and bedding, and I made a bed for us on the shag carpet with sheets and jackets and we rediscovered each other's bodies until the light came through an avocado tree.

Turns out it was a dumb idea, looking for summer jobs in June in a college town. We were laughed out the door most places and, discouraged and dejected, started living on a poverty budget. Riding our cheap bikes everywhere, shunning BART, and living off avocados and occasionally bread.

Jen and Hillary, who'd become friends by dint of being my exes, had found a Days Inn-looking shanty shack off Shattuck. But they had a TV and Jen had a job at a bakery, so to me they were like high society. Hillary had just grown hotter and hotter since we'd made out on the grass in freshman year, and I grew slightly obsessed with her even as I was sleeping with Pelin. Hillary started sleeping with Justin, anyway. Oh, the sexual tension that summer was pure and sweet, but thick as old Grandma Moses' molasses.

At least Jen and Hillary had that TV, and I was comforted every Saturday by Steve Harvey on *Showtime at the Apollo.*

*****

We were looking for jobs as busboys in creperies and rock'n'roll sushi joints or reading all day at Royal Coffee. Wandering the stacks at Cody's and Moe's. Bumming milkshakes at Jack-in-the-Box off Jen and Hillary, and staying out later and later to avoid Pelin, who I had started comparing with Hillary. Sometimes we'd go to Amoeba and there were shows at Epicenter in the Mission.

The light and air were different in a soft focus kind of way and the clouds went parallax, four to the floor, over the Bay Bridge, Sunday to Monday, never a break, never a cheap sleep.

So what did you do with all that wasted time?

Rode up and down hills on my bike with Justin, mostly. Or looked for sweet chill spots. I had this book from the Princeton Review called *Word Smart: Genius Edition* and made myself study it every day. And write poetry, late at night when Pelin had gone to bed.

And what else?

Seven miles from the old California heaven tree, I saw a sign that read: NEED A JOB? $10/Hour. I tore the paper off the wall and followed the tranquil streets like arid seas of light to a nondescript doorway off College and Shattuck.

Through the door and everything was gray inside, so gray it was shocking. A group of Hispanic teenagers and a slightly older white woman sat around filling out forms. A short lady in glasses with an unfashionable bob came out to greet me and handed me some forms. On the top of page one it read: Cutco.

"What is this place?" I asked her.

She said, "We sell kitchen knives."

"Oh," I said, and filled out my form.

It turned out her name was Jen, and she was the regional marketing director or recruiting director or whatever. She told us she'd started selling knives one summer during college and after college landed a fulltime job with Cutco due to her sales prowess.

The way it worked, she said, you didn't go door to door, you worked on referrals. So every time you gave a demonstration, you asked that person for the names of ten of their friends.

To myself I thought: I believe they call that sort of thing a pyramid scheme.

I almost walked out, but then she said something that made my ears prick up: even if we didn't sell any knives at all, if I could provide a list of one hundred names and have those people confirm they'd seen my demonstration, I'd get a thousand dollars.

And so my days as a member of the Cutco family began.

*****

They kept us in that gray room for ten hours at a time, like Russian defectors they were going to break. Showing us the demo over and over, making us memorize it word for word and try it out on each other. Taking us on verbal trips through long paeans about Cutco's famous Double D blade.

I started to giggle.

"The Double D stands for Double Durable," they said.

Ah yes. Yes, of course. My apologies.

My partner was a fellow named Andre and we almost cut each other's fingers off several times. It was a bonding experience.

I can't remember the names of all the different knives, but they taught us to cut the crusts perfectly off some Wonderbread and to do something with a piece of leather which escapes me. What really stood out to me were the Super Shears. A pair of scissors which also had the legendary Double D.

While we took the shears and cut the sides of a penny in circular fashion, we were required to tell a story about going on a picnic up a hill with a bottle of wine and forgetting your corkscrew. But you do have your Super Shears, and voilà, you show them the penny you've cut into the shape of a corkscrew.

I raised my hand and asked,"Who brings scissors on a picnic?"

So a symbolic three days passed and we were ready to go out and greet the world with our steely steely knives. I suppose I must have been somewhat brainwashed myself because I caught myself saying things to Dave and Justin like, "These really are pretty amazing knives."

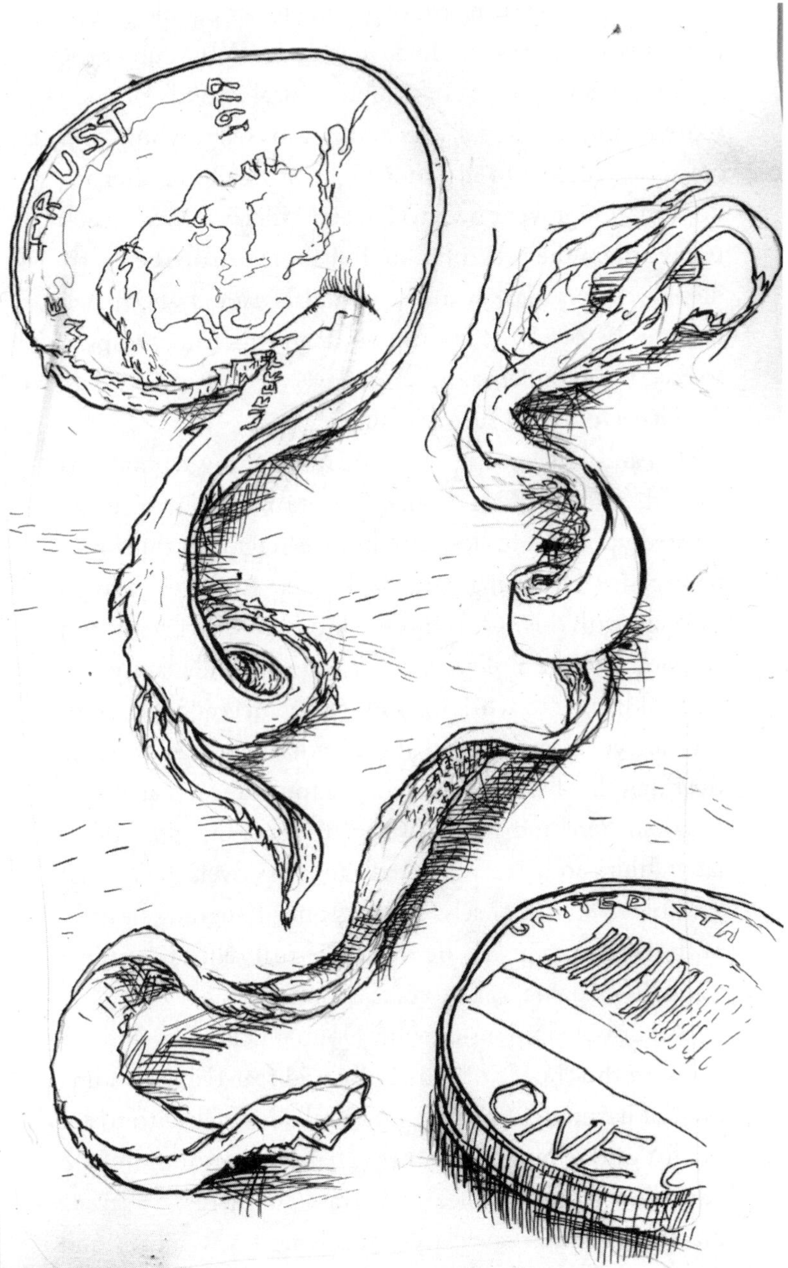
TRUST
ONE

And they'd give me those pitying looks people give to Jehovahs Witnesses and Dianetics dudes in the subway.

So I made the rounds of the local Goodwills and scored some ties and slacks and got myself a whole new corporate look. On my first night of freedom, after indoctrination, I went over to Jen and Hillary's on Shattuck to give them the presentation. For some reason the apartment was very dark, candle-lit, and I made it about two minutes before I cut my thumb open and crimson spray soaked the Wonderbread.

That Double D sure was sharp!

Jen and Hillary erupted into laughter, my wound was treated, and we all ate dinner. But meanwhile a voice had opened up in the back of my head asking: Can this really be my life? This thing with the knives? Am I really to go through with this? Or is this my life, here with friends and laughter and the ability to mock or forget the inanity and farce of having to work for a living and degrade oneself to this degree. Degrade? Is that even what I mean? Money is the thing that lies at the base of the foundation that allows us to sit here and laugh. When it is not there we don't laugh quite so hard. Will I have to cross over, then, cross the golden strand of selves to this one? Laughing heartily as the machines go. Knife man. The real self. Hello there sir, hello madame. Like to take a look?

All doubled up inside with Double D knives.

With the chords of self-doubt and fear rising in some kind of harmony, I set out not to sell knives, but to to get my list of one hundred names. That I had an aunt in Palo Alto was helpful; I took a silver train out there over serene marshland. And I saw my cousins Kingsley, Whitney, and Amity, all for the Fourth of July. And the vast irradiation of American endlessness, all bravos and clap clap on that coral night. But back to Berkeley was back to struggling in my own pale way up and down and even through the high hills above the old town.

So and so knows so and so. "Yeah, I'll sign the paper. Don't want the knives. Just show me the trick with the scissors and the penny."

Oh, lost one. Draw in a sigh. Numbers is all it is. Up and down the hill with a bag of sharp knives.

Meanwhile Dave and Justin had got even worse jobs working for CAL-PIRG and I went to a weird extension night-school poetry class with a nun in it. Figuring maybe I can pick up some pointers.

The poetry man, man of many vibrations, who taught the class was called Silverburg or Silverstein and ran a magazine called *Poetry Flash*. He'd comment on my poems that he couldn't comment on them. Whether that was good or bad, I wasn't sure. But he had a lot more to say to the nun than he did to me.

Improvising. Hard. Knew it a bit from jazz. Make the tune by not following, follow? Out and in and out again through the old fences and barriers and sour night pipe calls to get near that one naked thing.

Eye to eye. Night call and moon song.

Today they don't teach you that stuff much. Too right today is not always to write today. Anear, a fear, or about today.

In a minor key: something happened with my brethren at Cutco. They saw how many names I had and how few sales I had, and asked me to come along to a kind of pep-rally all-day infomercial at a hotel in San Jose.

So: me, Supervisor, my man Andre, and a Christian

woman just out of the army called Sheila. We all piled into Sheila's purple Toyota and headed out to San Jose. Had to blot most of it out but remember Sheila on the attack with Supervisor, who, being Jewish, was responsible for the death of Jesus. Andre in back, blotting it out with me. Wisdom all up front, Jesus on the bar.

They bore him lightly, they did, before they spiked him.

Sheila just back from the first Iraq, looking for a Cutco career and more words like that to the accompaniment of old radio slow jams, "Macarena" and "Wonderwall."

So San Diego. Home of the morning. Into a big convention room with all the other Cutco kids from the entire West coast. Felt vaguely like some Mormon gathering. Everyone for himself alone. A kind of roar. A silent one. Of salesperson desperation.

Trophies were given out to top sellers in their region, all the applause like too much blood in the ears. The wild thing was, I knew the top seller for my region. He was this hippie kid I went to college with. Turns out the little fucker had taken his mom's phonebook and called all her friends and begged them all to buy something. I found this out later over a stupefied smoke.

"What are you doing here?"

"What the fuck are you doing here?"

"I know, dude."

"This shit is crazy."

This hippie guy, Andrew, made enough money selling Double D's that he was taking off for the rest of the summer, trailing around Europe etc. etc. In fact, I don't think he ever came back. That's how good the hash was in Morocco in 1996.

Back to the convention room, charm-smiling again at the unswayed, the uncaring, the unforsaken shells of the Cutco crowd. The speeches began.

Tell us about the speeches.

There were long speeches, short speeches, speeches from ladies, speeches from gents, speeches from kids with lugubrious lips, grave speeches, painful speeches, speeches from the mountains, from on high, and from caves deep on the dark earth.

What did they say in the speeches?

They all quoted a man, a great man, it turned out. A teacher and a leader whose name was Zig Ziggler and he was teaching people, good Christian people, how to Take It to the Top.

Mr. Ziggler had even written a book called *Taking It to the Top*. And through the employees of Cutco, his immortal words lived on, like seeds planted in sterile hotel room floors to be nourished in suitcases and thrive in the homes of the misguided victims of their pyramid scheme, who had somehow learned to equate business with Christianity.

Jesus the CEO and all that.

The false priest's song, no voice of warning, sung to the tune of ten thousand kitchen knives clanking in an old fashioned Bethlehem picture puzzle.

I knew enough then to know it had started years ago with *Think and Grow Rich* and Norman Vincent Peale, and would go on past our P.O.V. here to transmute into the full-busted liquid gold communion of *The Secret.*

As the last man from the Cutco family told me, lights low, spirits high, in the spirit of an old-time seance and revival: TONIGHT, WHEN YOU GET HOME, IT'S JUST YOU AND THE PHONE. WHO'S GONNA WIN?

*****

Back to Berkeley with the same crew, chastened now with the holy spirit of the Double Durable. Sheila was on to Andre now about becoming a military man when I found a pamphlet on the floor and began to page through it in an attempt to remain invisible. It was a book about juice fasting. We've just come off the Bay Bridge, we're driving back into town, when the guy in the car next to us starts pointing at me to roll down my window. Huh?

At the light, I roll my window down, like what's the deal, man. And he says:

"Are you doing that fast?"

I'm about to laugh and shake my head when Sheila yells out:

"I am! I'm doing it!"

His eyes light up as he replies,"I did that fast for a month! After two weeks, my sweat smelled like spring water!"

*****

Crocus breath and a smile like an opera-glass folding into itself, Hillary, oh Hillary. That summer she decided she was a punk, and brought on the first of many riot grrl revivals with eyeliner and leopard print. She slept with my good friend while I lay awake at night, infatuated. Came out to find me for a cigarette and stayed up to all hours talking.

And the jutting bright stars faded.

With their tap tap tap came the dawn and its blue baton.

Pelin caught on and moved out and moved on and found the love of her life, San Francisco Jeff. So I didn't feel that bad.

I scribbled away and studied my *Word Smart* and sometimes, well, sometimes I'd lay out my big *Norton Anthology of Modern Poetry* and take a word here or there. Not yet a phrase, a sentence, a paragraph, or a page. But if I saw a word that I liked in someone else's poem, I'd find a way to stick it in mine. So I guess that open copy of old Norton was my gateway drug, when it came to the future's full-on plagiarism.

As the months turned with their sweaty music, July to August, sea-shadow and summer rose, my list of names began to flounder around fifty and I was nowhere near getting paid. So I found a job as a telemarketer in an office building near where they filmed *The Conversation*.

They put us at a long table with a bunch of old dial-a-wheel phones and a list of names and addresses, and we'd call these people and ask them questions about firemen. Not every question on the damn thing was about firemen, some of them had to do with local elections, but some firemen were clearly paying for it all, so every time we said "firemen" we had to follow it with the phrase "who risk their lives every day."

It made people laugh. I certainly could never make it through the whole interview without laughing. Occasionally I'd look across the table at some other poor sod, our eyes meeting in semi-quaver, and we'd both laugh, thinking "what the fuck are we actually doing here?"

*****

Jen had an older half-sister who was a divorcee and lived with her two precocious daughters in Berkeley. Hillary and I babysat, and they were delightfully smart little girls. Jen's half-sister Andrea was also a poet, but she had converted to some hippie brand of Orthodox Judaism and wrote poems about being a daughter of Abraham and Bathsheba and whatnot.

We'd struck up a friendship, had spent a weekend skinny-dipping in the woods with Jen and Andrea's boyfriend and had had some dinners together. One night, forgetting or unaware that I didn't drink, she offered me a glass of wine.

I hadn't been to a meeting all summer, just hadn't bothered to look, so in the parlance of AA was not sober but dry, and when she asked me if I wanted a glass, I said yes without the slightest hesitation.

It was torture. Soft and sudden.

Wonderful-feeling of course, to take a drink. But an alcoholic has trouble with just one drink. And the bottle was already gone. Now I could have said, "Shall we open another?" But the truth is, I would have drunk it all myself. Wallop. Gone. Pompeii.

So I left the banquet and walked home like a good salesman, dreaming of more alcohol. Just give me one of everything, please. But I was still underage. I'd have to go around asking people in parking lots to buy for me and anway I was broke.

Spent the rest of the night on the edge of wanting it and the edge of trying to forget I'd done it, praying up to the shimmering crystal roof, forgetful roof, glittering roof of the sky.

Almost had a year sober/dry and you went and done this, you did. Even worse, Big Al was going to be away all next semester in Amsterdam. So there'd be no big brother, just your lonely old self in that Midwestern land, that cold land of study and sacrifice and superabundance.

CHAPTER SEVEN

(a funny thing happens on the way to New Year's, the story of the mo's, down by the water tower, AC and others, whipped cream and other others)

I'd be living with Dave, Jen, and a woman named Jee-un Kim that year, junior year of 1996-1997, in the lordly pasturelands. The poetry anthology was coming out in late September, and I'd go back to New York for a reading at the Astor Place Barnes and Noble, but in the meantime I was the first to arrive at our new house. Every room was painted a different loud color, and the living room was red. Over the course of that year, in that red room, we would all lose our minds.

The previous tenants had left half a bottle of wine in the fridge. Having tried with great, deep-chested vigor to push the incident in Berkeley from my mind, suddenly here was the rest of the wine I could have drunk that night.

Who would know?

Or better: Who would know except me?

And, since I already knew I was a no-good, lying, self-justifying and truth-mystifying drunk anyway: Who cared?

I could live with the secret knowledge. Oh yes, with my wide-winged toughness, I could live with all kinds of secret knowledge.

So I drank the half-bottle and only got ever so slightly kind of buzzed. When would there ever be enough?

With a tear in my eye and a smile on my lips, I set out for campus, whose groves and dimensions I knew so well now they felt like home. Warm breath on my face, to be home again where it was safe. Safe to live in intellectual freedom once more, I thought, and no more knives.

But once again, I was still underage and felt silly going around begging someone to buy for me outside the convenience store as I had at eighteen.

I found my way to the Arb and lay down in that good-looking place with the tranquil blows and gasps of September all around me and thought one last time of Hillary, who would be in England all semester.

And then the school year hit me on the head like a lunatic caveman with a club.

*****

I only made it a few weeks before I downed a beer at a party when no one was looking. Then one night I took a six-pack home and drank it in my room while working on my poetry chapbook for junior workshop. Each poem was named after a different constellation but had fuck all to do with stars.

My professor, bless his soul, kept nudging me to clean it up a little, just focus, but I had grand ideas of a kaleidoscopic vision, even if I was only tugging at the wisps of it. I thought: The more I mess around the better, right?

I started sneaking into the disco on quarter beer night and professor beer afternoon and classical Thursdays for a nut brown ale. Mostly I'd manage to avoid people who knew me.

I was taking a lot of heat in general that fall: the kids in my workshops thought I was pretentious, I was hiding my drinking from my friends and housemates, and my oldest friends from freshman year were calling me a sellout for going PoMo all the way and ignoring them.

And they were right that I'd changed myself in certain ways to fit in. I was overly concerned with appearances.

At the same time, being PoMo to me was just being Mo. Mod stood for Modernist, right? Mods popped pills like French blues but we popped "happy trucker pills." Ephedrine was what eventually led me back to drinking full time. I didn't realize that I was already so wound-up with anxiety that all I wanted was to cut out the volupcy of the thoughts. Ephedrine made it easy to study and stay up all night, but it encouraged the thought-stream to spin off with orange rays to palaces on the sun.

Our common currency was really cheap beer and cigarettes and what had once been endless conversations about Saussure and post-structuralism, Jameson and Derrida, turned that year into slightly more endless conversations about Marx and Mao, Adorno and Horkheimer, and, if you were lucky, Raymond Williams. And though it was no doubt important to learn about bricolage and the Hegelian triad, I myself would not have lasted long without the cheap beer.

Steeped in levels of poetic and political thought of the very purest nature, I at last succumbed to full-blown alcoholism that November, at a party where we prank called professors and then ran naked through the library. I didn't wake up till it was dark the next day, and realized I was back.

Only cure when that happens is to drink more. Chase away one night's embarrassments with more, slightly more perturbed liquid embraces. Had I not been an alcoholic, had I been able to put down the beer and with light heart laugh about it all, it would have been a pretty fun year. We got up to some things, we did, but that beam of light from my oldest dimension kept squeezing round the door and through the keyhole.

But before it went all bad, I can remember:

- A short-lived band called the Wealth of Nations, in which we all played a different economist; I was Malthus, on electric bass.
- A guy named Doug leading us to this room where vodka bottles lined one entire wall like a shrine. Trying to leave this glass palace hours later and falling down the stairs and straight through the window of the front door.
- Getting together with a woman named Besa, who had a dragon tattooed on her right breast, and her saying to me, "I can't save you."
- Dancing around the red room with housemates to Sergio Mendes and Brazil '66.
- The red Farfisa organ in our basement.
- Spiritual essence of the nature of form and its deepest poetry, in the supreme and eternal vision of the naked image of Jackie L., former queen of Stuyvesant High.

*****

Contiguous or parallel to the times of human fun were other times rehung with badness, bad memories, and nuzzling regrets. By mid-November, everyone knew me to be off the wagon and I was drinking in public, going into blackouts and waking up in strange places, drenched with self-loathing and nausea.

Friends would ask, "Are you happy?"

And I'd say, "No."

But I *was* when I knew the prospect of drink lay around the corner. Cough-balls of excitement and new vigor would hit me.

"I thought you quit drinking."

"I started again."

Shame. Shame at existing. Shame of the belly button. Shame of the navel cord.

In the mornings I'd vomit while walking down College Street and not even stop. Got good at that. And I felt my skin beginning to soak it in, to smell like drink all the time. And cigarettes. It just clung to me in those misty midwest mornings.

But I passed all my classes and made it home for Christmas.

Hillary was on her way back to the States and was coming to New York for New Year's Eve. Dave was going to have a massive party at his folks' house in Montclair. Bands were going to play. Our band was going to play. It was going to be epic.

*****

The air outside the Dave residence is pregnant and glistening with rain and rain-dew, and the old house sighs quietly in its half-timbered sleep. It is five o'clock on New Year's Eve. An Isuzu Trooper the color of an oyster pulls into the driveway, and the doors clank loudly with youth-like ignorance.

QUENTIN: Think that will be enough?
DAVE: That's enough alcohol to last twenty people through the winter.
HILLARY: So you really are drinking again?
QUENTIN: I guess so.
HILLARY: Should I be worried?
QUENTIN: No it's nothing big. I'll probably quit again soon anyway.

Motion inside, laughter, setting up. QUENTIN *slings a look at* HILLARY. JEN *arrives and is handed a gin and tonic. Party of four, imbibing inaugural libations in the Florida room.*

JEN: Should we practice if we're going to play tonight?
QUENTIN and DAVE: We can wing it.
HILLARY: Who else is playing?
DAVE: Some band called 33-something with one of the women from Spitboy, and the Van Pelt, Chris Leo's new band.
QUENTIN: With Toko from Blonde Redhead.

Around them the room darkens as drinks are refilled, and the gondola skeleton of the old New Jersey abode creaks with danger signals as guests arrive.

HILLARY: You still haven't let me tell you about London.
QUENTIN: By all means . . .

As HILLARY *describes an affair in London with the organist for* QUENTIN*'s old friend Stew's band, who are now famous, the pair promenade the house as it fills up colorfully with guests and others. Greetings all around, new faces, old faces.*

HILLARY: Look at her.
QUENTIN: Leopard print?
HILLARY: She looks like she stepped out of 1995.
QUENTIN: She's probably in that 33 band.
HILLARY: Where's Jen?

QUENTIN, *lost in the bustle of the mob as it fills the house, wanders off, watches a game of pool, meets a curly-headed chap named Eric, and begins to lose consciousness. P.O.V. here is of the floor mostly: the wooden-metal secrets of nail to slat, screw to rivet, and a safari of parquet.*

QUENTIN: OK, you win.

. . . .

Time-lapse imagery of young twenty-somethings at a holiday party. Perhaps a Christmastime sweater here or there. One under the mistletoe. Two under the mistletoe. Half moon slivers through Venetian blinds. Camera finds QUENTIN *again, talking to the woman in leopard print.*

QUENTIN: You'rrrre cute.
DOMINIQUE: You're drunk.
QUENTIN: But am I . . . am I . . . a little cute?
DOMINIQUE: Maybe the tiniest, tiniest bit.

House opens up to a cross-section. As we follow QUENTIN *and* DOMINIQUE *to an empty room, our eyes also catch* DAVE *and* JEN *setting up musical equipment in the basement. One small Ampeg, one Fender Twin Reverb, one Vistalite drum set. One Fender Stratocaster. One hollow-body bass whose headstock reads simply: Maestro.*

QUENTIN: What's your name?
DOMINIQUE: I told you already.
QUENTIN: Oh, rrrright.
JEN: Should we go find him? We're on first, right?
DAVE: I'll find him.

. . . .

CUT TO: *Flex Lavender, the band, onstage performing. Pretty decently after all, as* QUENTIN *goes in and out of consciousness. Crowd seems into it enough until, for no reason,* QUENTIN *gets down on his knees like a heavy metal shredder guy. But he's playing bass. The bassist never gets down on his knees.*

. . . .

DOMINIQUE*'s band plays next.* QUENTIN *tries to stay conscious. Influence of toxins in his system and* *other phantoms, suggesting a juice-fast detox cure is in order.*

. . . .

QUENTIN: Who's this?
AYA: Chris's band. The Van Pelt.
QUENTIN: They'rrrre . . .
AYA: Good?
QUENTIN: They'rrrre grrrreat!

Darkness. As the other self takes over, the blackout self, ghost body, QUENTIN *rises from his seat in the basement and climbs several steps of stairs. Somewhere, the brain thinking: fuck-up fucked it up, fucked it up again, my mistake, I'll just go away now, on my own, with all my errors, see you soon.* QUENTIN *finds a room in the super-sumptuous chalet with its own bar and pours himself a gin.*

QUENTIN: That's more like it, Mr. President.

As darkness comes again, brighter than any man-made heaven, life-bright, as it falls over the pink flesh, the mirror shows us QUENTIN *fall in slow motion. As he drops, the skin to the left of the eye, almost on the eye, two millimeters away, hits the glass corner of the bar counter and opens up to a smooth spray of blood. The fluid flowing over his eyes and face until he hits the carpet, the great pale whale felled. And the red fluid continues to flow for at least an hour before two young lovers enter the room.*

LOVER 1: What the fuck?
LOVER 2: See that pool of blood? Go get that Dave guy.

. . . .

A small group of men is gathered to carry QUENTIN*'s 6'2", 190-pound frame through the rooms of the sleepy old house with its parchmenty half-timbers to a car, which takes him to the hospital.*

QUENTIN (*vaguely, to no one*): Don't tell my parents.
DANNY: Huh?
QUENTIN: Don't let them tell my parents.

Back to blackness, then through the doors, colossal bursts of sound, fluorescent lights, eyes shut. Onto a stretcher. Onto a table.

DOCTOR: He's lost a lot of blood.
DOCTOR 2: What's left of it has a really high alcohol content.
QUENTIN: Don't tell my parents.
DOCTORS: Huh?
NURSE: Stitches? Should I give him an anesthetic?
DOCTOR: Blood alcohol's too high. Just stitch him up.
QUENTIN: Huh?
DOCTOR 2: Don't mind us. Just doing a little sewing. That's right, close your eye. Keep it closed, that's right, just relax. Think of something nice, your favorite song, a family vacation, your . . .

CUT TO: *Morning and the mingling smells of the hospital washrooms and waiting rooms and the click clack of nails on a keyboard.* QUENTIN*'s eyes open. Where is he? Tries to move. Can't. Strapped down.*

QUENTIN: Where am I?
NURSE: (*garbled*)
QUENTIN: Can you please untie me?
NURSE: You sure about that, sugar?
QUENTIN: Yes, yes, of course.
NURSE: You have a way of getting home?
QUENTIN: Can you call me a cab? I know the address.
NURSE: I guess we can do that. But I think you're still drunk, sugar.

NURSE *rises and unfastens patient.* QUENTIN *shows his insurance card and is given a bill. Told to get stitches out in 1½ weeks.*

QUENTIN: Stitches?
NURSE: You'll see, sugar.

QUENTIN *tries to feel around the bandage over his left eye. Too much tape. Nurse hands* QUENTIN *a printout.* QUENTIN *reads printout in cab. Printout reads:* "You are an alcoholic. You should seek treatment immediately." *Duh, thinks* QUENTIN, *what kind of stupid diagnosis is that? Of course I'm an alcoholic.*

. . . .

DAVE *answers the door. Rest of house sleeps.*

DAVE: Oh no, you ruined your favorite shirt.

QUENTIN *looks down, half of blue Oxford is red.*

QUENTIN: Looks like tie-dye.
DAVE: Have you looked in a mirror yet?
QUENTIN: Should I?
DAVE: You might want to get it over with.
QUENTIN: Oh jeez.

In the bathroom with lights whispering and fans tranquilly blowing, QUENTIN *removes his bandage. The eye is blackened, as if punched, and two rows of stitches trace his eye around the frontal cranial bone.*

QUENTIN: I'm never drinking again.
DAVE: I wonder how many people are saying that right now?

*****

Hillary came to stay with me for a few days and we even slept in the same bed, but all my hopes of having her were dashed by the gruesomeness of my stitches and the battered flesh around my eye. So we made the best of it, went to museums and movies and shows and everywhere we went people stared at me like I was the bastard son of Frankenstein and Lucifer.

Eventually Hillary left to stay with another boy who had a crush on her in D.C., and Dave and I drove back to school in the dark and dead winter lightning for January term.

It was a voyage into the mind.

My stitches were removed at the school infirmary and all I had to do was read some books, but my brain was so blunt-angled it bounced off the page when I tried to focus. Took some time off the drink, tried to concentrate, wipe the old cobwebs from the eyes: still nothing. Could have been illiterate for all I was getting from, who? Maybe Cortazar. Probably *Blow-Up.* Used to be reading was like heat, eye to the keyhole, easy. Voyeur man was a fan of the nature of humanity and the mirror other humans placed to it. Now voyeur man have paralytic brain fizz.

It was a voyage into the mind that did not reveal very much.

But there were entertainments to be had out in the eventide cold at the expense of your dignity, drinking beers while people looked at you saying, "You look really bad, man."

Eye was still healing and I looked busted. My shit was retarded. And usually, that kind of a near-death, near-blindness experience would be enough to make a normal person re-evaluate a thing or two, but here I am out with the . . . well really a bunch of people I know hardly at all . . . the Viking heavy metal man with gout . . . and my old R.A. who seemed to have succumbed to the liquid turpitude as well, a couple of the lesbic ones and others, amiable enough, but wary of me, thinking to themselves what lies behind the machine that makes him keep ticking or is it only the flesh and serpentine veins that make the blood crawl. But what on earth is really making the young monkey go?

It was a voyage into the mind.

A prelude, an étude about nothingness and mirrors, mirrors held up to nature, and what happens when you try to stitch them together like a seamstress.

Dave and Andy now both had their girls girls girls, and other acquaintances too. But I could not hold up a candle to the mirror of nature without it mocking me, cruel nature with its suspended waltz of amber.

Thinking: How can I go on? The arabesque around my eye is the truth of who I am.

Thinking: My terpsichorean and thespian prowess notwithstanding, I have at last put the inside out.

Patterns patterns weaving weaving.

So I went on a voyage into the mind. It was the twenty-eighth day of the month of January in the ninety-seventh year of the century. I was at a party at Andy's house with him and others, and the light fused blue and the light fused white. It was severely cold outside, and everyone started dancing to get warm. Fused: *White light goin'*. Fused blue: *messing up my mind.*

But I didn't want to dance. Took a chair and inhaled my beer but I couldn't get drunk.

A mockery to the memory. I just literally couldn't get fucked up. Drank like twenty beers. But my shit was busted.

Everyone else was having fun and started yelling out, "Dance all night!"

"Let's dance all night."

I, in my armchair, overseeing the proceedings, took a voyage into the mind.

And I saw something there at last. Two words. Two words all women and men and children and perhaps even childhood pets know.

Two words?

I can't.

Pls. clarify.

I can't dance all night. I can't go on. I can't go on drinking.

Two words.

Why then?

Bitter mystery. They call it a white light. A moment of clarity. Which makes sense to me, it felt like clarity, like cold water on the face, cold fire to the intellect, saying stop. Stop trying to take voyages. You can't. You're finished.

No! No! What will that leave me? What will I be without my voyages, without my drink, without that inexpressible thing that I need, have always needed to keep myself separate from all of you? What will I be with the party raging and the clustered dancers so vocative and attractive all? Nothing?

You will be free.

But I . . .

Yes!

I can't.

*****

So January 28th, 1997 was the last time I took a drink. Big Al came back and I told him all about going back out. He said, "Let me ask you one question: Was it easy?"

And I said, "Yes."

Such a simple question, that made me realize the simple act of lifting a glass to my lips four or so months earlier had led me to a place where I couldn't look in the mirror.

I had reverse spirit-walked once more, crossed the golden strands, lost my center of gravity, my *omphalos*, all from picking up one glass of wine.

So we went and ate pancakes, then off to a meeting, and I got a sponsor right away, an architecture professor, and we jumped into the steps. And on that front, the craving went away quickly. I hardly even noticed it going. But there were some stars in my eyes at the time, and it was only years and years later that I would realize the obsession hadn't been so much lifted as transferred, moved along to other things. I do not mean to say that these other things were addictive, merely that the obsessive nature of my brain latched on to them the way it had on to alcohol: as solutions.

One of those things was plagiarism.

The other was called Katherine and she was my one great love.

2

good
Truth:
that silence that extended
years, I took to heart the
ent for everyone. Hadn't
Perhaps, on all fours one day,
wise, but back then I thought, mayb
make my truth something other than
And when the
back and
the thing that was
my interior like
spirit would leave with
gurgle
I could have my il-
lusions back again, the veil of *maya*,
were
desires in the daytime light. Desires for
approval, desires to write more,
more,
make
something great at any rate. No
*****
1997 turned into 1998, I turned twenty-one and had my first sober anniversary. I spoke for the first time: qualified, lead, at a meeting.
I puked before I did it.
I'd even written out notes. That's how disconnected from myself I was. Afraid I didn't know the insides of my own head.
Katherine and I had been having problems and I was very down on myself, feeling rejected, etc, embarrassed to talk about it, and I threw myself with new vigor into
120
"I'D EVEN WRITTEN OUT NOTES. THAT'S HOW DISCONNECTED FROM MYSELF I WAS."

CHAPTER EIGHT

(Katherine in winter and other songs on that theme)

Surely all personal history involves some great love around the age of twenty? Those eyes, that look, this gesture, that red hair, those gold freckles, this pale skin. I'd been struggling in the fresh pink flush of early sobriety where everything felt like freedom, and she stepped forward looking so very much like a nineteen-year-old red-haired Burne-Jones girl. I suppose we passed each other several times at night, in the library, downtown, all epiphanies for me, written on green clover, deeply deeply. All thoughts wholesome but of wonder, and a maze of questions. What was her name? Walking. Always proudly walking. From where to where? Feeling perhaps a bit of myself leave my body in the matter of the pursuit of these questions. Just a slight transference, as the days once more began to grow long and the sunlight came crude to College Street. I wrote a note. I wrote a note simply saying my name and asking if she'd like to have coffee. That way, coward that I was, I could hand it to her and run off. It seemed the only way. And when I finally did, she frowned at first, then her face lit up and it made me smile, but I was like a child now, counting days in AA, with no sense of how one did these things in the real world, and sort of waded and shuffled off hopefully, but already doubtfully through the frog green play-fields behind Rax and the old school to home, to home where I listened to *Sell Out* by the Who the rest of the afternoon and laughed to myself, not with any sense of conquest but at the memory of that change in her face and the white and gold that came out in it. The curls and curves of her mouth: pleased.

New air in my room it felt like, I put on "Girls eyes, butterflies . . ." and ambled about trying to read this or that, eye-skimming, and then out to the library or the dining hall, knew I'd see her somewhere, or her shadow at least, loping off ahead somewhere. Finally at the library she approached me on the long ramp and said her name was Katherine and yes, she'd have coffee and why not later tonight? So we went at ten for coffee at the Feve. My first surprise was she was from Los Angeles, like my father, but the Palisades, and the second was she was a voice major, an opera singer. We walked briefly around campus near the Arb, moon-schlepping, under the myriad dark-stars and it went unspoken I guess that we'd see each other again, but we didn't kiss. Our mouths didn't touch in fact for two or three weeks of night walks and conversation as the sky went violet and turned into outer space. She taught me about classical music and I introduced her to Hart Crane but was afraid to show her my own poetry, as sobriety had chastened me with self-applied lashes concerning the overall worth of the words I lay upon the page in those moments when I let my words lie. In that regard, the AA one, I had come to love the Saint Francis prayer and the Serenity Prayer and would say them not only on my knees but out walking or sitting on a bench as the writhing warm winds of spring came languid and reluctant to those midwest fronds. I had my sponsor Stan, Big Al, and several other men who helped establish the bedrock of my sobriety. Whether I was working the program actively or not, it never crossed my mind to pick up a drink, and that's because of them: Bill and Pete and Scott. Such good men, now fifteen years away or more from me in time and heart and the salt-blue of young memory.

As the days reddened and the nights brightened, I spent more and more time with Katherine or alone in the library. I'd discovered a section that was just shelves upon shelves of old literary magazines, bound together in wine-red hardcover editions. *New World Writing. Transatlantic Review. transition. The Paris Review.* It was all there, the history of literary fiction in the first half of the century as collected in periodicals. Parts of *Finnegan's Wake* as Joyce was working on it, same with *The Making of Americans.* In *Transatlantic Review:* British and American novelists and poets and playwrights from the sixties I'd never heard of, like Heathcote Williams, Gavin Ewart, B.S. Johnson, Giles Gordon, D.M. Thomas, Trevor Hoyle, Alan Lelchuk, Jay Neugeboren, Sol Yurick, Shirley Schoonover. Who were these people? I'd never heard of them. I was nearly twenty years old, foggy-headed in the extreme, sitting in a library, writing longer and longer poems that were beginning to look more and more like short stories, and here were these names, unknown to me and, I assumed, the rest of the world, and so their work began to creep slowly into mine. I started lifting passages from poems and short stories in these old magazines which I considered, or rationalized, to be lost to the dusts of time, in the days before Google and Project Gutenberg, when the Internet was just being born or in its goofy-faced adolescence. I took these words, stole them into my work. A library thief in the crossbeams and crosshairs of history's gauzy book memory, rationalizing it all: *wrong as right,* or maybe *just OK,* or *who's gonna know?* the general overtone and that's where it all began. The major emphasis in AA is on honesty, and there's a saying: You're only as sick as your secrets. The steps are set up so that after the first three actions of admitting powerlessness, asking for help, and realizing that help must come from somewhere outside of oneself, you divulge your secrets: you purge yourself of these things that could, potentially snag you up enough to drive you back out. I did my first fourth step at the same time that I was just beginning to plagiarize, and it felt like a new and wonderful safe high, a kind of easy and in-the-here-and-now ego boost, to show a prof or send to a magazine something so much better, more polished, and professional-reading than anything I could do, that I just wasn't ready to put it on that fourth step I did with Stan in his office that spring. The flowers and air and bolus locus of the season had filled me with notions of goodness and fresh starts and the sickness, the wrongness, the morally wrong thing I was doing in the act of theft, theft of intellectual property, word crime, was too dark to fit, somehow, into the framework of my pink cloud. I was getting good grades, there was color back in my cheeks, I was buying new clothes that didn't have holes in them, and I wanted it: the springtime, the innocence, Berg, *Wozzeck*, Schoenberg, *Verklärte Nacht*. The easy carelessness of life as a non-drinker, civilian, skin shining in the sun, without those dark corridors of mind and memory where I had lived on and off for so long, like a man with a time-share on Mars.

Meanwhile the band that Dave and Andy and I were messing around with, the Young Lords, became the Cocaine Nun; Thom Donovan and Nick Stumpf (later of the French Kicks) joined us, and we played one show at a house party in a crazy girl named Lena's room. She jumped up and down on the bed and hit her head on the ceiling and later accused Dave of stealing her ride cymbal.

Dave and I had begun to notice a pretty girl we called "the Washed-Out Girl" in our Chinese Cinema class. She had long black hair and ruddy skin, was perhaps half-Asian and always looked sad and tired. Several weeks later, we wandered into a party at a house called Shady Grove and saw her, the Washed-Out Girl, singing a song with acoustic guitar in a dark room where someone was crying. Her voice sounded wildly like Chan Marshall's in the days before all female singers imitated Chan Marshall. Later we found out her name was Karen. Karen Orzolek.

That that summer Katherine worked at the Barnes and Noble in Santa Monica, and I came home and got an internship at *The Paris Review*. She left school several days before me and so did my housemates, and I was alone again in that house with its strange red room. As though the year had never happened. I wandered the streets humming to myself, a song I'd made up about her, about my darling and please don't forget me dear darling, etc. Meanwhile, thinking: *The Paris Review.* Good career step, make good contacts, best lit mag out there, George Plimpton, will I meet him? and other things like that in memory shards scattered about my brain as it was growing in its gray-white way.

*****

The offices of *The Paris Review* were on Seventy-Second Street all the way east past York on the bottom floor of a massive townhouse. Mr. Plimpton lived above with his wife and young daughters, and worked mostly from there, in his safari-themed study, coming down occasionally to chat with the staff, who were all in their mid-twenties to early thirties.

Everyone there was brilliant and sarcastic. Dulled in the eyes in a way I would learn had solely to do with working in publishing in New York. But otherwise, attractive, well-spoken, and up-to-date. Brigid, Daniel, Anne, Steve, and James, who was down in the basement with me. Most days I'd sit on a bench that belonged to Mr. Plimpton's minivan and read unsolicited manuscripts. It was fascinating, and I could easily have done it all summer. I'd read these short stories unless there was some other chore to do. For example: fact-checking. They'd send me to the Society Library on 79th Street, a private library founded in 1754, to check statements made by authors in their interviews for the magazine.

I'll never forget the first one I worked on. It was an interview with the travel writer James Morris, who later became Jan Morris. I didn't know anything about the sex-change and it took me quite a while to get to the bottom of it. This was, again, in those dark sad days before search engines contained this kind of information and a young curious lad like me was sent trotting off to what they called the Stacks. Everything outside the Stacks at the Society Library was as you'd imagine John Jacob Astor's house to look. Then you went through a door and were suddenly in a dusty gray quasi-purgatory of old, mouse-bitten books and allergies.

Steve rode a motorcycle to work and, like everyone else at the magazine, as far as I could tell, he had a private income and didn't have to live on whatever "salary" he was given by Plimpton. Not that the magazine was hurting. It just tended to break even rather than make a profit. Steve was the first person I tried to talk to about the oddness of not only the slush I was reading, but the cover letters as well.

He laughed and pulled down a file they kept of the absolute weirdest cover letters they'd ever received. I added one of my own I'd kept, where the author had done the whole thing in Elizabethan-era prose. I'd made the mistake of writing him a rejection letter in the same style, which he took as encouragement and then sent more work with an even more ornate cover letter. Inside the folder, I found several letters from someone who'd written a story called "The Model-T Ford" but wouldn't send the story, just query letters over and over saying "buy my story."

There was an amazing poem I wish I could remember, on tropical stationery, that began: *New York Lady, slow down* . . . and then a series of letters from someone who claimed he was being held captive by the Dalai Lama, and that the Lama was "the goose that laid the golden egg."

Sometimes I'd talk to James, the managing editor,

about writing and he'd always say, "Learn that stuff, absorb it, and then forget it." Or, "If you really want to be a writer, get out of New York." Encouraging things like that.

About a month in, a second intern joined me: Fiona, who had just graduated from Williams. She was much more of a self-starter type and that left me more time alone with the unsolicited stories. Whenever I found something halfway decent, I'd think it was far better than it really was, because I was so used to reading such crappy stuff. I picked several stories that summer that I'd convinced myself were great, just because they were average, to show to Brigid and Daniel and Steve, and every one of them was laughed out the door. I really did hope to find something wonderful and surprising in the slush. But everything the magazine published came from agents anyway.

One day, Hunter Thompson called and I got to put him through to George. That was exciting. But otherwise I had very little contact with Plimpton, other than ordering food for him once in a while. I remember he really liked pea soup with croutons.

There were several readers who would come and do what I did, as volunteers, that summer. My favorite was Molly. She was getting her MFA at NYU and was always filling me in on New York gossip. She also told me one day she'd seen Radiohead the night before, this was circa *The Bends*, and had met the bassist, Colin. They later married, and she lives with him and their children in England. I remember that, sweetly, my mother would always pack me lunches, which I would eat surreptitiously while reading slush, and Molly would say I looked like a chipmunk.

That summer, in my free time, I'd see Dave and Andy and go to meetings on the Upper East Side, but mostly I got obsessed with writing a short story. I was reading so many of them every day, growing aware of their faults and their strengths, both structurally and spiritually, that I felt I had a good sense of what made one stand or fall. At James' suggestion, I'd gone and started reading all of Chekhov's short pieces.

When I finally did sit down to write my own short story, I employed the same two methods: I used the dictionary and my *Word Smart* book to insert random words and I used an old maritime travelogue for pieces of prose. Combined, I thought I'd created something of a made-up language, a kind of persiflage, that *was* readable but required some adapting to. It was certainly over the top, even if you didn't know it was all jobbed. Now that people know it is, its hard to look at it without it reading like one big cut-up. I also threw in some phrases from Baudrillard.

Towards the end of that summer, everyone got depressed and I saw Elliot Smith for the first time, at the old Knitting Factory.

Katherine and I had corresponded the whole time by old-fashioned mail: beautiful long letters in which our hearts and our intellects met at point infinity and fell to earth redolent of constellations and bispherical clouds.

I visited her in Los Angeles and met her family and went to the beach and her favorite cafes, but I couldn't quite place her there, as being from there, that house, that bed, those cats, that street, those hills . . . sighing . . . what and who had made her magnetic to me, this creature that I could only see as born of natural action like fission or fusion, whose epistles filled me with a kind of fully clothed love.

But we were naked together there. And we were naked together once more when she came to visit New York, and I took a week off *The Paris Review* to tour the place with her in those allotted days, relieved at last of romantic longing in relation to placation of desire, etc. I played her my song of June on guitar, and we both laughed at its awfulness.

Then one day, an aberration, my coffee consumption caught up with me and just as in my drinking days, only six months gone, I began to vomit while we were walking along the street on our way to Cold Spring. Wound up at the hospital. Couldn't stop heaving, and when it was all done they told me to quit coffee, take Zantac, and avoid acidic foods. Nothing was wrong internally. Well it was, but not in my stomach.

Given that I had my lovely gold-seamed and red-freckled girl, what was the matter then? Taking the wider scope? As my mind returned to itself, in sobriety, so did its fears, and this was the first one to cycle through the light cycle: intimacy.

In the midst of love, family, botanic gardens canoodling, sundials and sunsets on bulb and seed, I felt not smothered, but fearful: What if I am not enough? What if I cannot live up to what I am expected to be?

Moving, somehow, into the outer likeness of self-expression, opposites, and seeing inwards, intimidated by the deep hole there.

Inside: I saw only fear.

But there was something still to come: the recommencement of my secret-keeping about plagiarism did not help the old subconscious (where I ran parallel to my summer house-day self but with the augmented light of spirit kindling and all-embracing microscope eyes).

*****

After Katherine left, the nausea continued. I quit coffee for a week, thought I was dying, went back to it. The Zantac helped. Occasional vomiting on the subway, between trains, at the end of the tracks, where the lights flicker off like small night galaxies.

But dramatic force drove me back. Back to school for one more year, and early on received a call from Steve that George wanted to run my sea story. I'd sent it in to James and the younger staff had had mixed feelings, but George liked it. They cut some things and then didn't run it for two years. But in that time, the lead-up, I had the distinction of having a story out in *The Paris Review* while still a senior in college and thought to myself: Here I come, world.

*****

Unfortunately that meant pushing certain thoughts, night thoughts, away. The truth, essentially. I didn't know when the story would come out, and though I didn't find it likely anyone would recognize the words of Captain Voss's voyage that easily, *I* knew that I had taken them. The truth would come to me at night mostly, like William Wilson in the Poe story, and sit with me like a lost spirit in the room. It told me, this lost spirit, that I had deviated somewhere from it, from plain facts, and from the things, the terms and ideas we use to measure basic goodness.

I would ask him: William Wilson, is it that simple? Truth: good. Lie: bad? But there was no answer, and in that silence that extended over the selves of many many years, I took to heart the notion that the truth was different for everyone. Hadn't Einstein said so?

Perhaps, on all fours one day, I'd be convinced otherwise, but back then I thought, maybe I can find a way to make my truth something other than yours.

And when the light was back and I'd had some coffee, the thing that was burning up my interior like an acid spirit would leave with a gurgle and I could have my illusions back again, the veil of maya, because there were desires in the daytime light. Desires for recognition and approval, desires to write more, or steal more, to make something great, at any rate. No matter what it took.

*****

1997 turned into 1998, I turned twenty-one and had my first sober anniversary. I spoke for the first time, qualified, lead, at a meeting.

I puked before I did it.

I'd even written out notes. That's how disconnected from myself I was. Afraid I didn't know the insides of my own head.

Katherine and I had been having problems and I was very down on myself, feeling rejected, etc., embarrassed to talk about it, and I threw myself with new vigor into plagiarism. A novella with whole sections from the diary of a monk in South America. A longer piece with paragraphs from John Hawkes.

Now I wonder, since I did at one point have a voice, a little voice, where it went.

Did it lurk around sometimes like a phantom? Was it he who came to me at night?

What was it? The pressure I felt or thought I felt, to keep away from it? That it sucked? That it was true? Me? Doubly me?

*****

Katherine and I had been fighting and I grew jealous of anyone she spent time with. Oddly, at that very moment, as the spring began to come again and the earth made some music, a woman named Sarah started leaving things like flowers and orange juice outside Katherine's door at odd hours of the day and night.

Katherine liked it, no doubt, because it is nice to know someone has a crush on you, but also to stick the knife a little deeper in as far as I was concerned. Feeling of green. Feeling of Red. Slipping about campus, hoping perversely to eye Katherine with some random man or Sarah, to make sense of the change in her and us and what felt like something bitter and death-like. Secret to the touch.

Goodbye goodbye.

Sometimes we'd eat at the fancy Asian restaurant in town, where a classics teacher once asked if we were brother and sister. In my sweat-pursuit of aesthetic perfection, I'd been showing Katherine the "stories" I'd been compiling. And it was at this particular meal that she finally dispensed the wisdom I needed to hear but wasn't ready for, the truth and the nick of its rough blade.

She smiled slyly and said, "Why don't you ever write about yourself?"

"Wha?"

"I like what you're doing in this latest one, but wouldn't it read more authentically if you made it about yourself somehow?"

"Myself."

"Isn't it what most writers do?"

"Yeah, I mean, it's what they say, the old proverb: write what you know."

"It makes sense."

"To some, maybe. I'm not sure what it would mean for me."

"You have all kinds of stories. You tell me stories all the time."

"But there's no core."

"Sure there is, there's you."

"I'm no core. I'm like a black hole."

"Don't be silly. Everyone has a core."

"What would I write about? My childhood?"

"That's where most people start."

"Lame!"

Katherine, gaze crystalline now. "It's only lame because you're so obsessed with being different. You compare yourself too much to other writers."

All I could see was the flesh-colored blur of her head shaking as if to say: *Where did I find this guy?* Who looks so normal on the outside but is so darkly tangled with trouble, grave and self-willed trouble, on the inside. And that was when she realized, she told me years later, that she was always falling for underdogs.

I dug further into the literary journals of the sixties

and seventies. Those were the decades when people wrote sentences that had the ring of something otherworldly, like what we hear in the chime bells of *Tender Buttons,* but had added a slab of humor, like ointment, to those undersea sounds. I liked that best. *Motorman.* In the eighties was minimalism, which could work if the proper sentiments were buried, or just seem illiterate and money-mumbled.

So I stuck to my old names and even began branching out to textbooks and things as I began to envision a larger piece that somehow tied together Varèse's *Ionisation,* this notion I had that there were negative ions in the Santa Ana and foehn winds, and this sense I had that society was crumbling (of course!) and people were scattering away from each other like so many ions. Some basic concept, which in 1998 I thought was brilliant, that the heralded future of virtual reality and interconnectivity would bring about its opposite, and push us further apart, ultimately destroying us like Skynet in *The Terminator.*

My friend Thom had turned me on to Virilio, and his *Open Sky* especially had got me thinking quite a lot about technology, not just as this entity but as a metaphor (Heidegger had got there earlier) for how we view this mystic earthen realm. *Techne* and *Poesis*, Heidegger said, were our two approaches. *Poesis*: the planting of seeds and allowing the land to flower of its own accord. *Techne*: more like the process of mining, some invasive procedure to shape or conquer. It was a way of seeing, like the days of summer camp color wars when the old bird gods watched us in our green chambers of toil and laughed a warbled laugh.

When we were still together in spirit, Katherine and I had planned to go to Greece. Home of Perseus. Home of Theseus.

The root of Western Civ, I thought.

Whither goeth all great men, I thought.

Now that we were achy-breaky she decided to go to Italy to an opera program. I said, I'll go to Greece on my own and meet you there?

Perhaps, she said.

And thoughts of blue sea voyages filled my head. The geometries of early civilizations. Scanning them, turning them about in my brain. Even if not possible, penetration, perhaps acceptance?

Voyages of sea voyages filled my head.

*****

And then, in the weeks before graduation, when the earth was fat with green things once more, I cheated on Katherine with a dark-haired and pale-skinned Irish girl.

In my unaccustomed abstinence I had seen her around once or twice and stared at her in film class. She wore grandma glasses to hide how gravely beautiful she was and it was she, in the end, who left me a love letter in the campus mail.

I was writing about pears. There was a kind of pear called Anjou.

I had jobbed in a lot of stuff from Virilio about technology overtaking us too, but the story was really just about pears.

And it was spring once more.

The soil was fat with green things.

I was thinking: Pears the size of hearts, sweet with springtime sweat, girl sweat, ever so light like a thin fuzz above the lips or on the forehead you could just brush it away like silk.

The Irish girl and I rendezvoused in the unused courtyard of the humanities building one evening when everyone else was somewhere far. We drove in her car to a lake and she told me about the authors she liked and the stories she wrote and this one character she used over and over.

I thought: Character?

My word-thievery, my plotting, my planning and hatching had grown so abstract it was all simply words and concepts to me.

The notion of a character had never occurred to me. It sounded quaint and old-fashioned.

But I loved to hear her talk because the words came out of her like tiny lights that she had only discovered herself on the way up and she was convincing herself of them at the same time.

We didn't make love that night but we did other things in the dark. Or as the dark dropped its black hat around us.

But the following night we did until the morning came in violet and vain through crossbones of window. Pale skin and black hair like waterways flowing to freckled riverbeds, bury me here I am quite content. Connected as we are in softness: eye to eye, cock to cunt, where hair grows like flowers, bury me. And she did bury me, like a thrush. Like Brother Thrush in the pink and white waterways of those black flowers.

And it was spring once more.

CHAPTER NINE

(chants magnetiques, canvases of woe, in search of the puckerless persimmon)

It was as though I had walked through a dark, perhaps over-clouded corridor and come out in Greece. In Athens.

On the way they handed me a diploma, took a picture in front of a flag, and my parents and step-parents all hugged as they smiled then pushed me, hurriedly, through the tunnel taking people, impaled in their surprise, to the Aegean.

I said so many goodbyes.

I sat with Katherine in silence and in scorn.

She went to Italy.

Perhaps I'd come to visit?

And there I was walking through the dust-topped over-crowded rows of gray in the ghettos of Athens.

All summer I read *The Recognitions* – a book about forgery and fakery and Faustian bargains. Perhaps I lay somewhere in between Otto and Wyatt, but the irony was too good to be wasted on me.

After days of old pots and shards and wandering towards dusk through the burnished streets of Plaka, an older man approached me in Syntagma Square and tried to lure me down a dark alleyway with the promise of Coca-Cola and his love of America.

I left for Piraeus the next day. Slightly creeped, slightly overwhelmed, took the ferry straight to Santorini.

I was curious to see Akrotiri, the hub of Minoan society, north of Crete. On the ferry with me were mostly Germans and the only coffee was Nescafé. The light blue Aegean crested westerly around our wake, and I fell in and out of sleep, reading about plagiarism and falsification.

Our ferry landed near Fira and I took a bus up a hill. I was bombarded by offers for rooms from wrinkly old characters but knew roughly where the youth hostel was from studying the map, so I kept going. The rooms were co-ed and everyone was Australian.

The next day I followed some of them to the Moped rental shop. It was an excellent way to get around the island, all the beaches, and up to Oia, where I rode a donkey and felt guilty about it and picked an olive or two in a dry field one secret afternoon.

Everywhere was white-sharpened and blue.

But I was lonely sitting still and took a ferry to Crete.

I wanted to see the labyrinth.

I spent a day in Heraklion, where everyone thought I was German and yelled out insults I couldn't understand and then rode the bus south to Knossos. To see the labyrinth. I had loved the myth of Theseus as boy. The Minotaur. King Minos. Daedalus.

Icarus.

Our tour guide took us through the palace, which was remarkable and remarkably preserved, but when I asked where the labyrinth was, he laughed. The word labyrinth means "place of two axes." There was no actual maze, just a picture of two axes carved into a rock somewhere.

Overheated and depressed, I cursed myself for going all the way to Crete for the stupid labyrinth without once asking if it was actually there.

What had I been looking for *really*? Answers?

But the sea at Crete shone sometimes green, sometimes azure. And heading further south I found the beach at Matala, with its manmade caves that resistance fighters had used during the Nazis' airborne invasion. Later, they became a kind of natural apartment complex for hippies, including Joni Mitchell.

Unprepared for the heat, wearing cutoff shorts and black socks, with my face baked scarlet and my mind elsewhere despite the soft blue scenery, I took an overnight ferry to Ancona with a bunch of German bikers.

My mother and some friends had rented a house in Fiesole for the summer and I went and crashed on their sofa bed. Katherine was in Arezzo, and I went there during a bus strike and had to take a two-hour taxi ride.

It was wonderful to see her after my lonely time in Greece. She was in the midst of her program, however, so I went on to Rome, returned to Fiesole, and made plans with her to meet in Venice.

There, at last, I found my labyrinth and a kind of idle glory that overwhelmed but left me wanting. Or perhaps that was just my state of mind, or something sleepy in the air, or the force of gravity slowly sinking the place, or my fears about what I was going to do for the rest of my life.

*****

It had been more or less determined, though not out loud, that we'd have to break up in Venice. In Jamesian style. I was going to New York for a job interview at Penguin, and Katherine was going back to school. And of course we tried to relax in the sunflicker and unhasty agedness of the place, riding vaporetti and eating pasta meals, but the truth is it was depressing. Our hotel was too dark. Our bed was too stiff. We kept getting lost and stared at menacingly by old Mama Leones hanging out their windows.

The eventual narcotic effect of the labyrinth set in, and Katherine seemed not to care at all about me. So much of it I see now was depression, but I could blame myself for that as well, as the swing-doors swung and she swung away one morning, over water past those strange winding Christian minarets.

*****

World Cup fever had followed me through Europe that summer, including a wave-like ambush on the via Cavour, of mopeds and hoarse screams that nearly knocked me down. Now in Paris for my flight home, I had arrived just in time for France to play Brazil.

Everywhere I went, I was batted around by Eurostyle soccer hooligans in jutting colorful pennants and jerseys. American-style sports idiocy had finally overtaken the visions and dreams of the flâneurs.

It was what they wanted, in their hearts.

*****

Green with jetlag, the gentleman from New York, just back from Paris, took the time-honored silver train with the orange circle to midtown.

It was the height of summer and, liberally drenched with sweat in a light wool suit, he sat and waited at Penguin Putnam for a woman with a cropped haircut to usher him in and ask him questions that had, after tense expectation, nothing to do with literature or books and everything to do with typing speed and professional attitude. All seemed fine and serene, and then he was brought out to an old-fashioned typewriter and asked to type out a piece of prose on the subject of how much Penguin employees loved their jobs. But tired, fresh off a jet, and mobbed up in his mind, the potential secretary was not fast or efficient enough and long before the letter came, he knew it in his heart.

The applicant tore off his jacket and tie in the uppercut of the crosstown heat tunnel and a homeless man looked at him and sang, "This is Ground Control to Major Tom . . . "

Smiling, unwittingly, heat-drunk in another timezone, the young man decided to walk downtown thinking: New York again.

*****

New York, New York like a mammoth grazing in the cleft of bronze Catskill mountains and cedar fountain river Hudson. Murmuring flows mouldering down the West Side Highway past Tarrytown-Land of my stepmother's castle, land of teenage shame, gold-stepped Yonkers Raceway and Sarah Lawrence. Bronx exudes eagles, burns with poison, with pestilence. Where buildings sprout now in old weed fields, highways trespass against us.

The sovereign city growing unusually heavy in the purse those days, end of the century, after summer months millions in internet dollars complicating the lives of young college bumpkins. Lovingly combining code complications in the adjustable eye of history. Ocular and oculus omnivorous to the detriment and impediment of code-breakers anon.

They were pouring into the Lower East Side and taking it over. They were pouring into Williamsburg and renovating factories. They were pouring into Park Slope and changing the topographical definitions of its southernmost aspect. They were partially drunk on promises made about an interconnected future, and wanted to do their part. Recruitment for the silent war. Pseudo.com vs. Razorfish.com and so on. Plumage was multitudinous, and its outspread nature corkscrewed here and there for two years before it sank, painting the world latte-colored and reducing the bloody waves of each individual heart to microchip size.

Thank you, cybermen.

Thank you, Great Cyber Mother.

With no apparent objection from them or her, Dave and I set about looking for apartments and jobs and niches in which to make memories. Frank Castoria on Graham Avenue was our savior. He granted us a two bedroom on Grand Street between Lorimer and Union for $1000 a month, above a travel agency with a glowing yellow airplane. We moved in immediately, to that strange, slightly off-balance place and Dave took the big room and I got the small one, where my bed just fit and the light from the airplane took me on nighttime trips to foreign lands of human heat and animal.

In 1998 Bedford Avenue had the L Café, the Gray Parrot, and, nearby, Teddy's. Soon would come Vera Cruz and the Read, but it was nothing like the tourist's alley it is today. We would walk from Grand all the way to the L for decent coffee and breakfast. Las Palmas, near us, had OK espresso but also something called a Furkey Sandwiche and Tembleke, whose name fascinated me off an on until I tried it. If you walked in the other direction, Phoebe's Café had just opened on Graham and that's where everyone went from at least '98 to '02, by which point there were increasingly more options. Galapagos was the coolest bar around, with its reflective pool, but some liked to slum it at the GPT. Believe it or not, there were no legit music venues until North Six opened and, soon after, Lux.

Nearer to the Lorimer stop was smooth-worn and still not too messed up, except on Grand. Old Sicilian Fortunato Brothers and other bakeries and fishmongers seemingly not encouraged whatsoever by the "yuppies" coming in or, as some called them, the Village People. There was never a loving relationship between the Boricuas and the Italians to begin with, but in those first years, they did sort of unite in their common hatred of "yuppies."

In my three-button blazer and new-shined boots, I went to job interview after job interview with mostly nice, understanding women who worked in publishing. One editor at St. Martin's went so far as to give me a book to edit as a sort of test. I was serious about it and wrote what I really thought needed to be done with the thing and never heard from her again.

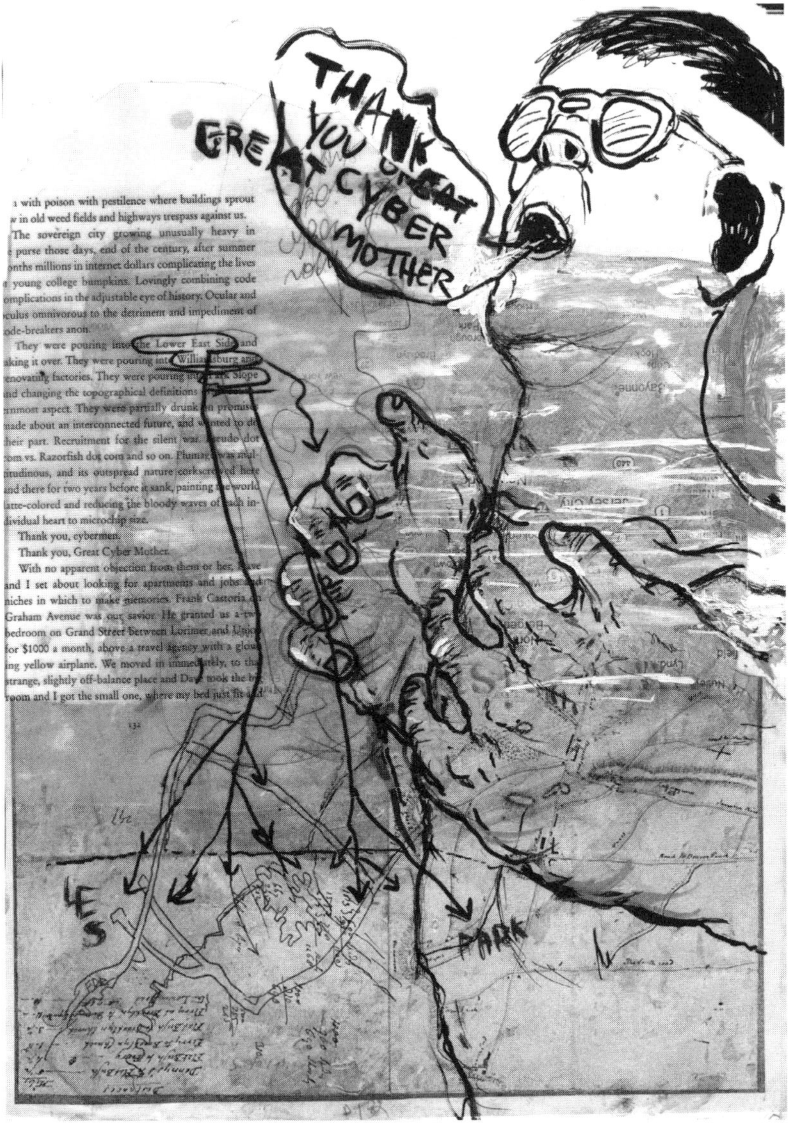

n with poison with pestilence where buildings sprout
w in old weed fields and highways trespass against us.
The sovereign city growing unusually heavy in
e purse those days, end of the century, after summer
onths millions in internet dollars complicating the lives
f young college bumpkins. Lovingly combining code
omplications in the adjustable eye of history. Ocular and
oculus omnivorous to the detriment and impediment of
code-breakers anon.
They were pouring into the Lower East Side and
aking it over. They were pouring into Williamsburg and
renovating factories. They were pouring in[illegible] ark Slope
and changing the topographical definitions [illegible]
ernmost aspect. They were partially drunk on promise
made about an interconnected future, and wanted to do
their part. Recruitment for the silent war. [illegible]udo dot
com vs. Razorfish dot com and so on. Plumage was multitudinous, and its outspread nature corkscrewed here
and there for two years before it sank, painting the world
latte-colored and reducing the bloody waves of each individual heart to microchip size.
Thank you, cybermen.
Thank you, Great Cyber Mother.
With no apparent objection from them or her, [illegible]
and I set about looking for apartments and jobs and
niches in which to make memories. Frank Castoria on
Graham Avenue was our savior. He granted us a two
bedroom on Grand Street between Lorimer and Union
for $1000 a month, above a travel agency with a glow-
ing yellow airplane. We moved in immediately, to the
strange, slightly off-balance place and Dave took the bi[illegible]
room and I got the small one, where my bed just fit and

132

*****

The waterfall of yes sir no sir eventually left me at the doorstep of a literary agency with a scouting division, on Fifth Avenue. Scouting was a foreign rights thing. Foreign publishers pay scouts to keep abreast of hot books coming out here, to get first dibs on them. Sometimes, this means while the book is still on submission at the agent level, but more frequently, when the book has gone to auction. Many of the books that did get auctioned off that way and made huge advances just sank without a trace when they came out.

They were all speaking their own language.

The big publishers that our agency worked for were Rowohlt Verlag in Germany, A.W. Bruna Uitgevers in the Netherlands, Emece Editores in Buenos Aires and Barcelona, and Tuttle-Mori in Japan. These folks all had star editors we had to kowtow to, and when they visited give them rockstar tours of the city. My boss was a smoker like me, and we were always getting yelled at for smoking in the office by the woman who later sold *The Da Vinci Code*. After Carol was Ariane, the daughter of the founder of Rowohlt. She'd had the Nabokovs as babysitters when she was a girl.

Books would come to us; we'd read them overnight, write a report, and send it on to all the clients. The only book I recommended that ever got bought was *Slackjaw* by a guy named Jim Knipfl. A few days after I sent my positive report, Thomas Pynchon blurbed the book. Our Germans bought it and my boss said to me, "Enjoy it. That's as good as it gets in this business."

*****

They liked me as a reader but loathed me as an administrative assistant, and that was largely my role. It was a violent and skin-deep immersion into the world of phone/fax machines, copiers, messengers, Fed Ex pouches, Pitney Bowes machines, conference calls and filing, filing, filing. I had my own company email address and used it mostly to write bored joke emails to my friend Hannah, who worked around the corner at the Internet start-up Kozmo.com. The idea there, I believe, was they were an online video rental and delivery service who slowly branched out into delivering just about anything and then were destroyed by UrbanFetch.com, who in turn were destroyed by Amazon.com and Netflix.com.

But before the Wrestlemania of the internet giants truly began, places like Kozmo existed everywhere. Most of my college friends worked for them, got stock options and their own business cards, and went to strange internet-startup-only mixers where other future guardians of the ether were in evidence.

Internet dollars helped the art world go and the real estate world go and Williamsburg continued to be renovated, though not built upon yet because not re-zoned yet, so artists could still afford to live there, next to the web designers who supported them. Meanwhile the publishing world struggled, not as it does now but as it did before the chain-store freeze-outs and Jeff Bezos's brass knuckles. There were names in New York like Coerte Felske and Kurt Anderson and *Run Catch Kiss* that one had to learn. Our clients had wildly different tastes from your average American: their biggest U.S. authors were

I LOVED IT! THOMAS PYNCHON
brought up plagiarism as one of my character defects, but
ositioned it so as to seem something farther off in the
st. He was comforting and we talked about much of life
especially in music, in film, if not yet so
istence itself seemed a kind of plagiarism
my character defects and found tha
be congenitally unlovable. Even w
my mind was still working over
e more.
this could be the case with plagi
t: ambition. Ambition to be
follow through. In that se
big payoff without the
e to see it more as
hinging from its
tly impress,
mile, was go
may not b
I sure do
roblems.
his house thinking:
y own truth.
SLACK
THIS IS AS GOOD AS IT GETS

Maggie Estep, Colum McCann, and Stewart O'Nan.

So you'd occasionally be caught having to nurture their delusions that, *Ja*, these were very popular authors in the States too. *Ja, sicher!*

In the room next door to me was Nelson DeMille's agent, and down the hall was Nicholas Sparks's agent, and these too were great men, to be spoken of in only cathedral-appropriate tones.

Despite myself and my friendship with Big Al, who had moved to Amsterdam, I fell for his ex-girlfriend Hannah, she of Kozmo dot com, and we slowly fell into a brief, mostly physical dalliance that was amazing but felt illicit and quickly devoured and spat us out. Hannah was, within her movements and possibilities, easily the most beautiful woman I have ever known.

So like a swan.

And she would ask me in bed: Do you like me because I look like Katherine? And I would laugh and say no, I like you because you are you and so like a swan.

She rented a room in an apartment on 14th Street that belonged to a family – cheaply, in return for watching their kids. Making love there, late, we'd have to cover each other's mouths to keep from waking the family.

In so many ways it felt new, like we were new, in a city where we could be new, that newness was a kind of flood of illumination that would rid us of our hazy memories and antediluvian selves.

But the ghosts of Big Al and Katherine floated like blind planets around us in our runaway time, and finally Hannah told Big Al and that was that.

She left me for someone with a job at the *New Yorker*. But there was always something or someone new to come ferociously along to distract me.

Other things besides the internet improvement people did exist, after all. There was music before The Strokes. There were bands at Brownies and TISWAS at Don Hill's, and Shout!, everyone's favorite Mod dance party, Sunday nights on 13th Street. That was where we rediscovered Karen Orzolek, now Karen O, a fiercely different creature now. She had become an extrovert, a character, and Dave and I were both temporarily smitten, though I imagine so were most dudes in that small window before the Yeah Yeah Yeahs and fame, when she was a mortal like the rest of us. Once, she gave me her phone number and asked me if I was circumcised or not, then drew a giant cock under the digits. And once, I ran into her at the old East Village Books and she kept laughing, and when I asked why she said she couldn't stop farting.

*****

I hadn't talked to Katherine since Venice, and it was a source of regret and historic blame associations within my own psyche – when out of the blue and into the black she called me that winter and invited me out to breakfast. She had transferred to Columbia without a word of warning. We met at Veselka for raspberry pancakes and she looked wonderful. She seemed like the Katherine I first knew once more.

She was taking classes with Gayatri Spivak and excited about that. It was brief and hopeful in the spirit of would this be a step forward or a step back?

What followed was a dinner at Café Gitane, where we embraced and kissed and it was so intense we had to take

MY NUMBER

a taxi all the way uptown to her dorm at Columbia so we could make out the whole way.

Making love once more with her in the familiar dark, on the Upper West Side, in the hour of the moment of the time of the era of the alabaster ice cream queen, was splendid and familiar, with hips and dark and bosom.

Her body once more responded to mine, did things of its own, intrinsically compatible proportions unlike the original so like the memory.

Waking up strange in a jacket and tie to go to work, not in college, in reality, thinking: Could the foothold of our private humanity take foot or hold in this place so unlike the old? Where everything is displaced by its newest model and I myself at twenty-two am already obsolete?

*****

Weekends we'd spend reading at the old Hungarian pastry shop. From Gaddis I'd gone to McElroy, most brilliant and unsung of systems novelists, within or without the strange loop, whose sentences suggested number-music and information extending over quixotic truths and contingencies to land once more in the footsteps of the real. After him I craved more long novels written intelligently in the shadow of Joyce and Lowry with invincible sentences and confidence trick plots.

For a while I dallied with Vollman and Powers, went back to to read the DeLillos I'd skipped, found Will Self and Martin Amis, the short stories of Denis Johnson, but slowly felt my options dwindling, maybe Murakami, maybe Knut Hamsun in *Hunger* or *Mysteries*;

finally I found my way back to the original perpetrators: Hawthorne and Melville. Children of the Revolution.

*****

We were a perfect match in those days: Katherine was an opera singer who'd lost faith in her own voice, and I was herding myself to the library to steal the works of other writers because I'd forgotten if I had one.

All around me colors of the world changing, days burrowing into themselves, minds opening liberally under the eyes of the world wide web. Thinking: Keats was already dead at my age. Thinking: Rimbaud was trading arms in Abyssinia. Thinking: maybe Hawthorne had it right. Holed up on a room at home for ten years, did nothing bur write and even then hated *Fanshawe* so much he had it torched after publication.

Thinking: Who am I, snivelly snot of an impoverished snail, that I even deign to compare myself?

Who am I to begin?

To begin was to remember. Still have story coming, sea story, in *Paris Review*.

Was to begin to chase that, well, dragon in consternation and premature decay, to steal more words to fit my ends.

Begin again? At the grand old age of twenty-two?

Words I remember stealing at this point from the Brooklyn Public Library Grand Army Plaza branch of my childhood belonged to writers Scott Bradfield, Jim Lewis, Paul Cody, and others and others and others in pieces never published, later self-published. Nothing doing.

Nothing doing.

Down the old house-field rows to the F train to the G train back to my box on Grand Street, wondering, was I paralyzed mentally? Had I merely petered out from the attendant fears of work, money, apartment, relationship? All widespread in their emotional whereabouts and commanding of concern. No more room to dream. Because once, even, when I was a word thief, I could still write this or that bit to make it all work and now: nothing. Theft alone.

Drying up.

*****

We went to Schoenberg's *Moses und Aron* and Katherine wore a lightly billowing gown in the early spring evening, and I wore my usual blue suit, and we walked downtown to Lincoln Center with the chrome-bone reflection of the moon in the windows on Broadway.

Running late from work I'd forgotten my bag and carried my copy of *The Ice-Shirt* in my hands. Katherine seemed to disfavor this and asked me if I'd ever read a thick, complicated novel that I hadn't liked.

"Of course," I said.

"Like what?"

Nothing sprang to mind.

She sort of raised her eyebrows in salute to the truth of the question. Sun-warmth falling at a slant on the color-points of her soft features.

"Can't think of anything I've really hated. I mean what are the parameters: The Bible? *Moby Dick*?"

"No, no. Twentieth century. You know the kinds of books I mean: *Gravity's Rainbow, Ulysses, The Recogni-*

tions, Women and Men, Infinite Jest, Under the Volcano."

"Those are like my favorite books of all time."

"I know. What I'm trying to ask you is why?"

"Because they're complex and interesting."

"Not because they're show-offy and geared to impress by overwhelming the reader?"

"Oh come on."

"It's such a closed loop. And it's exclusionary."

"Huh."

"Maybe that's part of the appeal to you."

"No way. I like other kinds of writing too."

"You used to. You did when we first met."

"I still do."

"I like writing that tries to communicate rather than obscure."

"Sure, of course. But reality can be quite complex and there are so many different ways of experiencing it."

A certain vacancy had come over her face, a kind of theoretical skulking, and I knew she was thinking once more: My boyfriend is a pretentious idiot.

*****

That was my only year of suits and ties and subway-style respectability, and when I was eventually fired it was hardly a surprise. Electrifying it had been, months earlier, to play the role of the adult commuter with the look of the man in the upstairs apartment, affection regarded, off to work and doubtless whole. But I had run into problems in the actuality of the work substance. In the end it was as a yeoman, or my yeomancy to a phone/fax machine, that destroyed me.

We kept an apartment for visiting dignitaries from the republic of Rowohlt Verlag and one of them could never get the phone/fax to work. So they'd send me over and I'd press a button and say, "There now you can send a fax," and leave. But later, when it was time to make a phone call, he couldn't because it was still on fax. So I'd go over again and switch it to phone.

I'd receive angry phone calls, "Niko says the phone/fax is still broken. I thought you said you fixed it."

"I did."

"I just don't know if I can trust you anymore."

But in truth, it was the simple matter of a button. A button to press. So simple, in fact, no one would ever let me explain.

I said my goodbyes to the opulence and Ariane and professional etiquette and Nicholas Sparks and office-tide symmetry and Nelson DeMille and scurrilous carpentry and Coerte Felske and fax machine mudslinging and Jhumpa Lahiri and wandered down Fifth Avenue with a cigarette in my mouth and a smirking twitch in my eye thinking: Score one for the machines.

*****

I wandered down to Perry Street, where there was an AA clubhouse with meetings all day. That afternoon I got a sponsor named Brian, who was a singer and the president of the Steely Dan fan club of America. His approach to AA was Californian. He'd had a sponsor himself who'd had many years and then gone out, and when he came back decided he'd missed something crucial in the Big Book. So he spent much of the rest of his days making an annotated version of the Big Book, which defined every word. For example, the word "sanity" in every context it's used. Needless to say, his version dwarfed the original book, and there were only so many copies in circulation. But Brian apostolically started a private (nothing in AA is private) Big Book study using his Study Guide. It was a weird scene, and most of us eventually bailed. But I liked Brian a lot and even learned to play all his songs on bass at one point. But there was never a gig.

The lodestar of his philosophy regarding AA was that anything I did wrong had to do with what he called *Self*, by which I believe, he meant *Ego*. The purpose of AA was to *Get out of Self*. That was it.

If I came to him and said: I'm disturbed because I just lost my job and don't know what to do now, he'd say: Sounds like good old-fashioned *Self*.

It was confusing. In those days, my understanding of AA was confused because of this notion that if I had to always be getting out of it, my *Self* must be inherently wrong or twisted. And though, obviously, it *is*, to view my *Self* only with scorn and distaste and never with love or understanding or compassion leads back to self-hatred, doesn't it?

Had I seen then that I could substitute the word *Self* for *Disease* or *Alcoholism*, I could have skipped years of casual depression and acting out. For if I separate the part of myself that is my disease from the part of myself that is just simply me, I can see there is some good there. Certainly my disease – my fear of not getting enough or having enough or being good enough – confuses this, and can easily turn me into someone with no principles whatsoever. But if I am working the program and focusing on the maintenance of my spiritual condition, suddenly I find I *am* outside my disease.

Eventually, I began to find that certain situations required more nuanced advice than *Get out of Self*.

*****

Katherine went back to the Midwest to finish school and it was fine, really. We'd fallen out of love once more by spring.

*****

That summer I went to visit Big Al in Amsterdam. He had a squat all to himself on Schinkelhavenstraat and was studying with Frances-Marie Uitti, who was famous for playing the cello with two bows. He and I had corresponded extensively about what had happened with Hannah, and I wasn't too worried about us having any kind of big confrontations.

We decided to take a road trip through Scandinavia.

Having only been to Maastricht, I was bowled over by the sinuous and nimble maritime brick beauty of Amsterdam. We spent several days there buying tents and sleeping bags and getting our rental car together, a bright purple kind of smart car.

I enjoyed the day air and night air, reading at Café Vertigo in Vondelpark and watching the street life in Leidseplein. Reflections maneuvered along the old canals and candles chink chinked with wineglasses in outdoor cafes harpooning the bridges.

There were hip-shakers and heroin addicts in the red

light area, which I wandered through sort of accidentally on purpose and ran away from in a hurry after a massively large woman stepped out of her window and exhorted me: "Come back – am I too much woman for you?"

*****

The idea of north was the idea behind our trip, so much so that we finally stopped, high above the Arctic Circle, in a town called Å. It was symbolic enough for us, at least.

I remember that through Germany to Denmark the people became more attractive, the driving more civilized, and the scope of things more human-sized. The sky darkened later and later, and Copenhagen and Aarhus were fine cities with rare forms and throngs and pleasant gestures in the air. Fragments of Sweden were farmland and red houses. Stockholm, a wonderful city, especially Gamla Stan and the Viking Ship Museum. Öland looked fantastically Bergmanesque, and ferries and other night ships carried us through the Baltic, emptying out on midsummer lawns. Northerly winds took us through Lapland and Oslo in the rain, and Bergen blinking in the screened hour. Through Hamsunland and Hammerfest and the moonlike land of the Samis to Nordland, Nord-Norge, a world of fjords and gray air and fairy people, descending the stalks of ice mountains to hunt sea-geese and Americans.

It was there, near Narvik, that Big Al woke me one night and asked why I hadn't made a ninth step amends to him about Hannah. I thought I had, in letters, and in conversation my first day in Amsterdam, but I suppose it wasn't enough. And I wondered why, as a person who

IDEA OF

was always apologizing for himself, why was I never any good at the big ones? I made amends to him, tried my hardest, but two separate minds aren't always able to see a thing the same way. We can only see the world through our own eyes, I know. Some of us, silly us, like to try to play ventriloquist is all. Just a little matter of pitching the voice through the darkness.

Through the darkness of morning we took down our tent, saw the small fishing village of Å, and headed south. Our moment of conflict was at the apex of Freitag's triangle, which made it a perfectly symmetrical narrative. Once we turned around, we headed south quite quickly.

All that intimacy had freaked us both out.

*****

Bye to Big Al and back to New York meant looking for work. A new bookstore had opened on Bedford, in Williamsburg, but they were only hiring cute girls. All around town with resumes, I got a job at a crappy place in Park Slope called Booklink.

Weird crew, learned a bit about ordering new books, but the system was old, Booklog, and the distributors were junky, Bookazine. Main memory is that everyone but me was making a horror movie together. Also a deranged customer in a beach hat did me the "favor" of reading the entire *Tao of Pooh* out loud to me.

Got recruited from there by the manager of the Community Bookstore just down the street. It was a much nicer bookstore with clearly, a much brighter staff and owner. I switched over sometime in the fall, with just enough time to train before the Christmas rush.

There was a really disheveled dude named David, who later started this lit mag called *Unsaid* and turned me onto some good shit. He'd been in Gordon Lish's workshops with Lipsyte and Marcus and Lutz and all those other dudes and ladies who did good and fun things with language that was coming out of that crummy old eighties style but had a little *Tender Buttons* and a little *Motorman*.

Sunspots that year.

Also there were Rich and Ryan. Roommates, one on methadone, the other struggling with heroin. Ryan came to a meeting with me, went out, and eventually got sober at home in Marin. Both big on puns. Rich was sure that Dave Eggers, who used to deliver *McSweeney's* by hand, had stolen some joke for that big book he wrote.

We all went to see *Dude, Where's My Car?* in the theater on Court Street, and that was the highlight of my year that year.

After some months, Cathy, the manager of several years, bought the store from the previous owner. Cathy was a character, with a mess of curly brown hair and a love for authors like Thorne Smith and Anita Loos and the guy who wrote *Auntie Mame*. I believe she saw me as a brother-like figure, but I was always slightly puzzled, decoding her proclamations and soldiering on.

Just as I'd got a handle on ordering with publishers and distributors through Anthology, the odd, expensive software we used, Cathy took off on a road trip to Texas.

CHAPTER TEN

(police paranoia, A tale of two Nicks, foreign correspondent/alligator man, JJ, Summer Gold, incredible shrinking . . .)

Working at a bookstore had the curious effect of making me not want to write, try to write, steal, whatever it was I was doing, at all. The presence of so many colorful and fantastically bound, lovingly crafted items made me feel useless and unworthy. Part of me, however, was fine with this notion that I could be the keeper of the books rather than the maker of them. Willingness to take trips to the library for stolen passages serpenting away from me now, "creative" urges vulturing away from me now, man-shaped shadows of early failure fluttering away from me now, I said yes to an offer to join a band my old friend and former girlfriend Jen was forming with her brother.

We were called the Wolves and, later, the Eaves. Jen sang and played guitar and organ, and Nick played guitar, and a great Oklahoman multi-instrumentalist named Casey played drums.

We practiced in a basement in Dumbo that always flooded, and recorded a demo of our first four songs. We sent it around and the booking guy at Brownie's offered us a record deal on his label, Ace Fu. Turns out he was the curly-haired guy named Eric I met at Dave's New Year's party when I almost lost my eye. Anyway, they'd put out some notable acts at that point, including Pinback and the Ex-Models and Ted Leo. We said yes right away.

Having the deal in place before we had really discovered ourselves as a band put a kind of pressure on us that took away all the fun and made it all about success. Casey and Nick had some weird rivalry going on. Casey really wanted to play guitar and convinced us to kick Nick out of the band. After that, we were always trying to find a decent drummer.

Our earliest shows were the best, when the whole NY rock thing was still, well, a thing. Brownie's, with the French Kicks and the Yeah Yeah Yeahs. Karen O told me I was the Incredible Shrinking Man. Lux, with the Fiery Furnaces, who were also flirting with Ace Fu but held out for Rough Trade. Knitting Factory, with the Walkmen. Bowery, with Ted Leo and Weird War. But there were many, many awful shows including a heavy metal band with all wireless gear at North Six, and something called Shitstorm.

Our first tour, with new drummer Tim, was opening for Damo Suzuki, legendary singer for legendary krautrock band Can. We were going to rendezvous with Damo and his people in Chicago, playing one show along the way in Rochester.

The place was called the Bug Jar, and we set up our stuff and went off to eat at a place called the Atomic Eggplant. When we got back the first band, the Earl Cram Revue, was on. Two dudes with no shirts and leather vests onstage and a slightly obese woman with glasses, singing. But she wasn't onstage – she was wandering around the room touching people's faces, saying, "Please forgive me, guys. I just got out of the emergency room and I'm on all kinds of painkillers," and then singing, profoundly, "Innocence is an emo-oo-oo-tion!"

The crowd at the Bug Jar loved us. Especially Casey and his "psychedelic guitar." We laughed about it and couldn't wait to get out of there, with the notion that only brighter things lay ahead.

Stuck in traffic outside Chicago the next day, we were informed that Damo had been deported. Or rather, he'd never had a proper work visa that would allow him to tour.

Slightly in shock, we decided to soldier on with the tour. But all the venues kept canceling, and eventually we gave up.

There were some very *Spinal Tap*-like moments, playing massive venues to literally no one. We had two fans of our own show up in Michigan, but the sound man talked to us through the monitors the whole time we played, saying, "Homey's got to tune his guitar." Or, "Homey better turn his bass up."

It was an exercise in futility. Playing to three people made us all realize we weren't really in it for the fun at all, were we?

*****

Quashed in ego and dreams of musical success, I returned to Brooklyn with nothing to do for several weeks. Most days I'd stroll over to Perry Street in the West Village or other meetings in other locales, but I remember my multi-colored wanderings in the West Village best because that's where and when my short story "Bethune Street" came about.

A kind of wide-leaved and wild-weaved nostalgia would hit me whenever I passed Bethune Street. It was Cross's old street and I'd never go down it, to avoid the museum of sticky-sweet high school memories.

But one day I did, dared myself to walk down past the blind masks of the brownstones and D'Agostinos and maroon haters and change-makers and lollipop kids. They in their fraternity and I in my lovely confession box.

That was the lost time. Uncovered again all instants, turning away from West Street, turning away from Eighth Avenue, unheeded against the chambers of silence. Unheeded against the bank towers of old Fourteen and the fluke trees of Abingdon Square and the lilac trees of Hudson on the Hudson. That was the lost time. That summer, no work, no band, realizations of uselessness coming in double-decker and shear-thudding. Fucked.

So fucked. Only good with a word when it isn't yours. And there, there on Bethune Street, nape of the neck tingly, you can at least admit that you have lost a little. How old are you? Twenty-four? Twenty-five? Thumping along in dissolution through jaundiced afternoons at Perry Street with wet-brain Todd always begging from you and following you, and hell, I even shared. But can't share the truth, can I? That was the lost time. Symmetry of it all incipient. On the back end of the parabolic curve. Eyes running to grass. Remember your words, teachers, profs, remember Cross, what would she think of you here. Returning, by way of the mystic afternoon hours, the morning consciousness planes.

*****

But the notion of being this creepy guy who never quite got over his first love stuck with me, as I am a basically nostalgic person, and that turned into a story about someone like me who finds himself hanging out around his old school looking for some sort of apparition or reincarnation of his first Cross, whose name was Emma Brown. And it takes a handicapped girl, wounded on the outside as he is wounded on the inside, to help him move on.

"Bethune Street" was my last foray into plagiarism for several years. I had the story distinctly in my mind, but it was visual. Of the words: I was unseeing. I was cold and dirty blind. So I'd try to start . . . Fielding walked . . . Fielding stopped . . . Fielding thought . . . And something circled in memory. Always had a memory for text, where a certain word or passage lay within a certain book and two came to mind: *Brideshead Revisited* and *Our Man in Havana.* From Charles Ryder: *Love had died between him and the city . . . here my last love . . . there was nothing remarkable . . .* And from Greene: *Little flower . . . old rampart . . . repulsed with heavy loss.* Both war zones: Ryder coming upon the old house in the war, Wormold pensive . . . therein lay Fielding. Some combo of PTSD and Salinger meets once more Waugh/Greene-esque religious longing.

As I proceeded to put the work together (I can't say "write" it), an old book by Janet Hobhouse became handy for some of the basic scenery and moving Fielding from

OF THE WORDS. I WAS UNSEEING
I WAS COLD AND DIRTY BLIND
SO I'D TRY TO START. ALWAYS HAD
SOMETHING CIRCLED IN MEMORY.
SO
I WAS COLD AND DIRTY
BLIND. ALWAYS SOME
THING CIRCLED IN MEMORY

point A to point B, while passages from Stephen Wright's *Going Native*, a fantastic book recommended to me by Lorin Stein, then still an assistant editor at FSG, were used for pyrotechnics.

I'd done something similar the last time I'd tried my hand at a short story, using lines from Nicholas Mosley's *Impossible Object* and combining them with longer passages from William Gass's *The Tunnel.* (There was always this matter, which will seem laughable to most, of finding works that fit together stylistically in plausible ways.) *BOMB* published that one. They are wonderful people, Betsy and Lucy, and have an intelligent, vital magazine, and I will never forgive myself for deceiving them or the great Frederic Tuten, who introduced us.

It was *The Paris Review* who published "Bethune Street." This time around, I actually sat down with George Plimpton in his office, to go over the cuts and changes he'd proposed. Of course I felt honored to be sitting there with him and found his insights into how the piece should flow remarkable, but I was deceiving him and the rest of the fine people there. Part of me, the part of me that wasn't under the clutches of denial, was sick with what I was doing.

I remember looking in the mirror in Plimpton's bathroom, thinking I was decomposing like a corpse with the silent shape of my mendacity a kind of whiteness, white silence, spreading everywhere and corrupting everything I touched. The man and the magazine, who had been so kind and plucked me from obscurity, and all I was doing was passing back along the shape of my disease, white and polished.

*****

Dave had started playing bass for Ted Leo and the Pharmacists – was a Pharmacist, I suppose – and always gone on tour. Our subletter was a friend of Dave's from Verona, New Jersey, named Andy. Andy was a writer and worked at Alabaster Books on the old Book Row. He and I, somehow or other, wound up writing two screenplays together. Working with a partner freed me somehow from the bonds, looping and grave-like, of plagiarism, and we were able to have fun. Mostly I was the idea man, the concept guy, and Andy was good with dialogue. Both screenplays were comedies. The first was a high school sex comedy that was also a monkey movie. We called it *Valedictory Chimp*. The second, *The Last Touchdown*, was a Melvillian college football story that was really about quantum physics.

Nothing ever came of the work I didn't plagiarize, and both screenplays live somewhere in the whispering death-chamber of Andy's files with so many of his brilliant, perhaps too brilliant, short stories and novels.

As Ted Leo continued to grow in popularity and Dave slowly turned into a rockstar, I threw myself into work at the bookstore with new abandon. There were customers to please, myriad-minded and variegated in their interests and profanities: Old Reverend Robinson, the Captain, Morris, Dave H, Gray-Haired Lady, Nancy, Mean Lady, Mean Lady 2, the Twins: Raphaello and Donatello, Rabbi Old Guy, and the dogs.

Cathy came back from Texas with a mangy dog who liked to sleep in front of the entrance, tripping everyone upon arrival. Her names was Priscilla and the syllable "Pris!" sounded out like mountaintop chimes for years to come. Soon another stray dog with a hair loss problem came aboard. Then came the dog food and waterbowls spread around the store. Then came the health inspector to close the store's cafe.

A woman named Lynn became the manager, by dint of having a loud voice, and decided I was a problem. I knew about books and all the store procedures, and could therefore be a threat to her. So she decided not to talk to me.

Cathy and Lynn bonded over a mutual contempt for the world. David and I hid in the back and talked about Kiss and Cheap Trick. He'd say things like, "If Tom Petty and Thom Yorke had a baby it would be Nick Gilder."

Or: "You know what the *OK Computer* of the nineties was?"

"*Crooked Rain, Cooked Rain*?"

"No way, man. *Siamese Dream.*"

"I can see that."

"You know Lennon was going to record an album with Cheap Trick?"

"No way."

"Yeah, but Yoko thought it rocked too hard."

Everyone was so highbrow that no one could ever recommend mysteries or thrillers or YA books. So the weekend manager, John, and I took it upon ourselves to become versed in these fields. I took mysteries and thrillers.

First, since our clientele was mostly female, I tried to cover the basics, like P.D. James, Ruth Rendell, Elizabeth George, Val McDermid. All the names we sold the most of. Then I moved on to the men, particularly enjoying Ian Rankin, Reginald Hill, and John Lawton. Having only read Poe and the Holmes stories as a boy, I'd missed out on the phenomenon of the sympathetic loser detective and all the technical dazzle that modern forensics and communication technology had brought to the genre.

Then I went backwards, to noir, and found that I preferred the slightly deeper and certainly creepier psychology of Ross McDonald to Chandler or Hammett or Cain. Ross McDonald's families were like my own, with a splash of Macbeth. Lew Archer had a mind like R.D. Laing crossed with Albert Camus and Bob Hope, devoted to finding the one partial fingerprint in the place it could never actually be, while recognizing the absurdity of the action.

I was a convert.

I no longer wanted meandering, sentiment-based storytelling, unless it was Derek Raymond or David Peace. My notion was that the contemporary novel, apart from strict practitioners like McEwan and Ishiguro, had been drawn down to the level of the voice piece or the opinion piece that could glide along on the eccentricities of its narrator.

I only wanted plots.

I only wanted *The Day of the Jackal.*

And I pitied myself as I couldn't pry my gaze away from the sight of the wound. Point A of any mystery always beginning with some small dishonesty and spiraling outwards to take others into its circuit.

Or: the vortex that lies within any human heart.

Around that time, Penguin reissued Ian Fleming's

James Bond novels with vibrant, illustrated covers.

I started with *Casino Royale* and went through them all in order.

I was hooked.

So different from the films. So much more bizarre and at the same time suave, the wonderfully epicurean descriptions of meals and clothes and hotel rooms, alongside the perversity of torture and random ultraviolence. More to do with Calvinism, Freud, and the French New Wave, I thought, than the quippy Aston Martin gadget man of the films.

I took an airplane through solar rays and the clave of clouds.

I took an airplane to Japan.

And I read *Moonraker* and *You Only Live Twice* in Tokyo cafés where the fashions seemed to have come from the outer ring of the world of James Bond, as if deep within the vortex of any human heart, on the outer ring of the twentieth century, Ian Fleming had created a mirror which eventually danced past its own shadow.

*****

After "Bethune Street" was compiled I got a new sponsor. He was the sound guy at Mercury Lounge but later went back to school and became a doctor.

With him I repeated my fourth step, and in my fifth I brought up plagiarism as one of my character defects, but positioned it so as to seem something farther off in the past. He was comforting, and we talked about much of life being mimicry, especially in music, in film, if not yet so much in books.

Sometimes existence itself seemed a kind of plagiarism.

We rooted out my character defects and found that I believed myself to be congenitally unlovable. Even when I knew I was loved, my mind was still working overtime to make you love me more.

I could see how this could be the case with plagiarism. I had always thought: Ambition. Ambition to be the best without the artistry to follow through. In that sense like gambling. Going for the big payoff without the money in hand for the bet.

With Jason I was able to see it more as fear. Fear of being useless or worthless, hinging from its staple to the obverse, needing to constantly impress.

Jason had a wonderful smile, was good with words, and I left his house thinking: I may not be able to quit this plagiarism thing just yet, but I sure do have a handle on a lot of my other problems.

But I also left his house thinking: Echoes, echoes, and the disparateness of my own truth.

*****

I was set up on a blind date with a woman whose name meant "honey bee" in Greek. A pixie-like hairdresser from California, we laughed at the same things and sometimes for different reasons. She was a bit older and her folks were giving her "where are our grandchildren?" vibes most frequently. In that regard, I felt some pressure to settle, when everything else in my life was unsettled and thus, couldn't really think about it.

Before the woman whose name meant "honey bee" in Greek, I'd taken a year off of dating. I'd had some

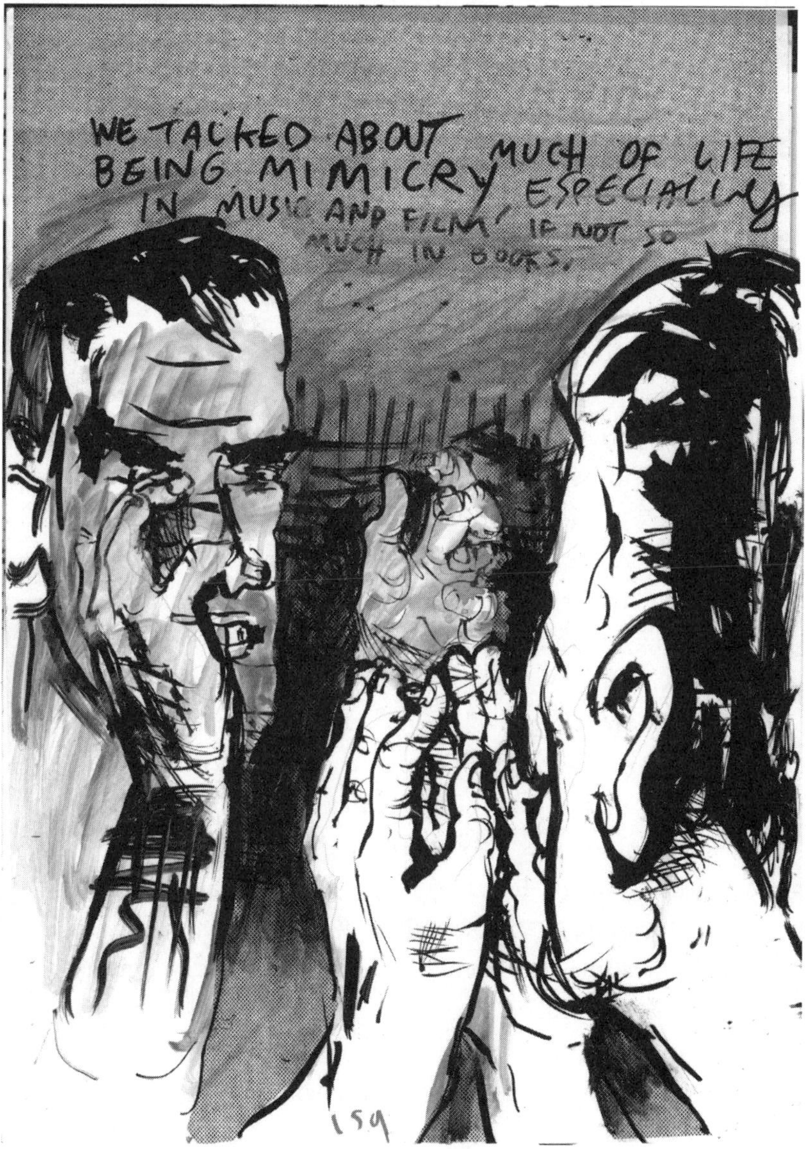
WE TALKED ABOUT MUCH OF LIFE BEING MIMICRY, ESPECIALLY IN MUSIC AND FILM, IF NOT SO MUCH IN BOOKS.

disastrous experiences with women older and younger, who all seemed to feel that I'd been put on this earth to ruin their lives. To which I could only say, "Gosh I'm sorry. I'm just unsure of what I want right now."

With Honey Bee our common language was movies, and there was a year or two with her when I saw every major movie that came out of Hollywood. Unfortunately there are only so many movies you can see before you have to start talking.

That was always awkward for us.

She was a good and kind and pretty person, pure and simple, with one side to her and no mirrors. She wanted to get married and have children, and I didn't know how that would be possible with the kind of money I made. She gave wonderful free haircuts to all my friends and came to all the Eaves' shows, even the bad ones, like the one at Lit with the collapsing stage where we played all our songs double-slowly as if several hundred feet below sea-level.

Why do I feel such regret and such shame when I think of her? Why, for instance, couldn't I have branched off, like Plastic Man, to go back to LA with her while the rest of me was in New York. Or, in stratifications of time, all geologic-like, lived one era with her and returned later for more to the parenthetical stones? Or, in regards to some space-time penumbra, slipped though a kind of dimensional pinhead to an inverse California with only subtle memories or flashes to the ever-moving component, New York reality, in which I had finally figured out how to earn a living?

Dave (who was always on tour with Ted) and I moved in with his girlfriend Sarah, into a fantastically wooden apartment. Once more, I took the small room, but it was a nicer small room, with a higher ceiling, and the clean, family-like feel of the place, combined with Honey Bee, combined with the fifth step, kept me away from plagiarism for a while.

My life became simply a blur of bookstore characters, bad movies, cable TV, and Sarah's half-Siamese cat Bond.

I would come home from work cranky, and Bond would paw at my door till I let her in and fall asleep on my stomach.

Phases. Phases.

Sarah was an excellent baker, and Dave a very good cook. They did domestic things together, like homebrewing and gardening. And I thought: Oh yes, this is how people live their lives, isn't it? The union of male and female at the matrix, radiating outwards to successive phases of domestic affairs, ceremonies to mark time, time in life, dishes, floors, levels of internal loyalty, outward respectability, and on and on to the break of dawn.

I worked at a place where my boss let the local crazy lady sell her cookies in our cafe.

And I was with a woman I did not love. And though I admired her a great deal, to express my mind, to express a notion – through no fault of hers – was not always possible. Misunderstanding leads to tears, leads to: *Are you breaking up with me?*

No, no, I was just saying . . .

She was kind to animals, to the spirits of animals. And it was through her cats, Rocket (RIP) and Lucy, and Sarah's crafty Bond, that I too became a lover of animals and the strong, good spirits of animals. Animals, who absorb our suffering and transmute it. Rocket, Lucy, and

Bond: antidotes to suffering, such feminine supremacy, such delicate perfection, to allow us to look on them and even touch them.

And though I always laughed at a friend of mine who used to have an Afro and got all into "healing" in college, I do believe, I do, in the glorious spirits of animals.

Amid the slightly vacant questioning pose and equivalency of these days I describe was a sense of general decline. A) falling out of love or lust or grace with the woman whose name meant 'honey bee' in Greek; B) the increasing weirdness surrounding me at the Park Slope bookstore, evidenced by the morning my rollerblading boss called in sick. I said: What happened? She said: I was up all night in the park, chopping trees for new bookshelves. *Prospect Park?* I asked; and finally C) the complacently melting center of our band, as evidenced by the loss of another drummer and other Fleetwood Mac-style shenanigans.

Can I bring all three of these with me through the pinhead? That oh so salient dot, to tell you . . .

Yes?

To, uh, tell you . . .

Tell us what?

I had a nervous breakdown when I was twenty-seven.

CHAPTER ELEVEN

(talking 'bout this and that and the other . . .
talking 'bout chocolate pudding . . . talking
'bout Mrs. Dracula and some other sad spirits)

I thought I was dying. The sweat, hair slick, heart atmospheric. Honey Bee took me in a cab to the hospital place, waiting gray, waiting green, finally: it was a panic attack.

Oh snap!

Are you sure it wasn't something with my heart? It really felt like . . .

No, it was in your mind.

My . . . ?

Your mind made your heart race that way.

Daisy chains of thought-worries?

Defective chains.

Profound fear sparking profound fear in consequence of defective deficiency?

Mind chains, yes.

Night thoughts?

Your body is telling you something your mind hasn't grasped yet.

I am afraid?

You are depressed.

No, that seems too obvious. Can you modulate?

Mixed or unmixed feelings in accordance with life situations, wanting that, not wanting that, something not fitting, something not right, body telling you . . .

Weigh the disorders?

Honey Bee, Job, band.

Word theft? Nah.

Take this, it's called Ativan. If you feel like it's happening again, just take one more. Carry it around in your pocket.

Is it addictive?

No.

Because I can get addicted to anything.

You shouldn't have any trouble.

*****

But I did. The Ativan was too good. Made me sleepy. Home and work: safe places, mostly. Outdoors: something oppressive about space.

Acceding to the requests of parents, went to therapy. Went on meds. Funny, really, at seven years sober, thought I had my shit together and AA was all I needed and then *boom*, look how much I wasn't allowing myself to see, feel, or process. Just to make it through the day and say fine, fine. Everything's really fine. And I had been fine since I was a child. First lie I told.

Buried then I was. Deep within the onion.

Ten thousand layers to this thing called Man.

Therapist said: *Remember.*

I thought: *Remember?*

Remember your parents' divorce, *remember* the anger and how you absorbed it, *remember* the new faces, the remarriages, *remember* their anger and how you absorbed it, *remember* your step-siblings and their anger and grief and how you absorbed it, *remember* your stepmother and how she beat you and her own son and threw you out of the house, *remember* your father, perhaps unsure of what was happening but there still, *remember* the taunts: you're fat, you looked like a girl, you were a faggot, and later the muggings, the weapon blue, sideways, sun-glancing, remember the watches, Walkmen, jackets stolen, meaningless, of course, but to *remember* the question: *Why me?* And *remember* your stepbrother saying it's something about your face. You mean, I'm asking for it? I don't know, something about your face. *Remember* the recognition that the world would physically attack you if you looked a certain way. *Remember* efforts, attempts to look different, to be different so grown men wouldn't punch you in the street and groups of kids wouldn't surround your bike with Exactos, and cars full of grown men wouldn't chase you through the silent streets at night saying, it's something about your face, *remember* to *remember* that the world really was only a Spider-Man comic, in the realization that there *was* evil in the world, there were adults who abused, competed with, and beat, with hatred in their hearts, on defenseless children who were too young, having not yet read comic books, to understand the concept of evil and could only *remember*. Even sometimes when it got better, you grew tall, having to go off and just cry for a while because there was no one you could tell without seeming like you'd lost, like you'd done it wrong somehow, ghosts in the basement and love can kill you. *Remember* always: there is evil in the world, superheroes aren't real, no one can protect you from the inevitable cold Tantalus fists of your own family. And *remember* always: ghosts in the basement.

And love can kill you.

*****

Therapy was helpful but like opening up an abandoned grave that I had long ago decided wasn't mine anymore. There were sores. There were scrapes. There were maggots that appeared, and spirits I thought I'd outrun long ago.

So: the idea was to no longer run but to feel.

Feel? That whispery fuzzy dusk-like thing that tickled your neck and vanished?

I managed, somehow, to feel my way out of the relationship with Honey Bee and out of the crumbling edifice of the Eaves, and shortly after that, the bookstore too.

*****

Oddly enough, in those early days of therapy, before the meds had hit, I was mugged. Three men jumped on top of me from behind, at two in the morning on a quiet street. I wrestled them off until two of them pinned me and the other got my wallet. Once they were up I chased after them, called the police while running, the police car intercepted me as I ran, and we caught them about ten blocks down still running. All I wanted was my stupid cards back. But they'd taken the cash and tossed the wallet. We never found it.

Later that night, at the station, it turned out the ringleader's name was William Wilson. Just like the character in the Poe story.

*****

When the medication hit my brain a few weeks later, I found it was impossible for me to have a panic attack. For that alone, I will always be grateful to the big pharmaceutical companies, even as they ruin the world. If I tried to go off the pills, once more the oppression of space, the collision of luminous axions, and dendrites not being re-uptake inhibited.

And one day, one of the owners of the bookstore in Williamsburg near my apartment offered me a job.

FRESH STARTS

His name was Miles, he was the son of a well-known art dealer and had put together a breathtakingly eclectic store with his best friend from childhood, Jonas. We had a meeting, several meetings, and I remember Jonas was fascinated to know how we ordered books in Park Slope. It turned out they didn't have an inventory system. They wrote everything down on paper and used an old-fashioned cash register.

NEW TIMES

On my first day, I swept up a bit and Miles told me I was already better than his other employees. I laughed, figuring he was kidding.

CHANGING THE SUBJECT

There was perhaps a bit too much testosterone in the air at times at the bookstore, but it was far more enjoyable than Park Slope. The clientele was younger, for one thing, thus much less prone to treating you as a servant.

SYNTHS AND CIGARETTES

Everyone smoked or was trying to quit or trying to start again. Sean was such a heavy smoker he'd palm his cigarette and walk inside the store with it to help a customer. Before Bloomberg really settled in, I mean as a concept more than as a man, we all smoked in the back room and the bathroom.

FUNNY HOW THE DAY GOES

Perhaps it's the stuff and only the stuff of retail, that one day weaves into the next like an injection of yesterdayness until a year has gone by.

FUNNY PAPERS

Miles and Jonas both had their aggro sides but were also funny and usually reasonable people. We were all New York kids. And we were all obsessive. I'd taken on a fair amount of the ordering, but they each had largely opposite notions about what and how many books to order and I was always being torn one way or the other.

FUNNY PAPERS REVISITED

After some time in therapy, on meds, with a new job, I felt the need to create something returning, but didn't want to steal, especially after my visit from William Wilson, and flailed around for a while until I started drawing again. My mother had taught me how to draw when I was tiny, and though I mostly did superheroes back then, the basics of anatomy and proportion, etc. – you never lose those things. So I thought: Maybe I could do a comic or a graphic novel, and that way there'd be less text and I'd be less likely to steal?

HORSES

It was thrilling to set about doing something that would be entirely my own, and oddly enough, I had a story all mapped out. It was a true story. And slightly epic, if I could tell it right.

HORSES 2

My father's mother's father, William L. Brann, owned horses and had been Eugene O'Neil's roommate at Northwestern. Betty, my grandmother, grew up at the tracks: Pimlico, Saratoga Springs, etc. When she was seventeen or so, she eloped to Cuba with a kind of playboy character she'd met at the tracks. Her father sent a man down to fetch her and take her out to Las Vegas to have the wedding annulled. Betty's father saw Louis Rowan Sr., my grandfather, at racing events, and they struck up a deal. Lou Sr. would marry Betty, and in exchange he'd get two of Brann's best brood mares. So the deed was done and done again. Lou Sr. grew up in Pasadena. His father, R.A. Rowan was a real estate developer and had built much of downtown LA. In fact, these days you can buy yourself a fancy condo in the old Rowan Building on South Spring Street. R.A. married a woman named Laura Schwarz, and they had several children together before R.A. dropped dead quite young, from booze. Laura took my grandfather and the rest of the children to Europe for boarding school, and while she was in Switzerland, met an Italian prince at the Deauville spas. His name was Prince Domenico Orsini and he was the papal nuncio, the prince consort to the Pope. Shortly thereafter, Laura Schwarz became Princess Orsini and my grandfather and his siblings all bathed in the light from the golden bowl. When Orsini died, Laura returned to Pasadena to the old family seat, modeled after a Stuart castle, and eventually Lou Sr. returned to help run R.A. Rowan and Co. and invest in race horses. That is the world that Betty stepped into: Los Angeles in the early forties, a strange old mansion with a strange matron who wore only black and was referred to as Princess Laura or, later, by my father as *Grand-mère.*

SO

In a different world, I might have been an Italian prince.

THEN

During World War II, my grandfather was with Patton in what had formerly been the cavalry. One of the things my grandfather had to do was rescue a cluster of Austrian show horses called Lipizzaners, from a depot in Czechoslovakia, and ride them into upper Austria. Patton knew the fellow who took care of these horses from a previous Olympics, and agreed to the mission because they were both scared the approaching Russians might capture the horses. The war was not over everywhere as the Americans rode the horses out of the East.

YEARS LATER

One of my grandfather's horses made it to the Kentucky Derby in 1966. The horse's name was Curious Clover and that is what my story, my graphic novel, was also called. But his Curious Clover, the star of the West, had only run on dry track. It rained in Kentucky before the Derby, and Curious came in second to last.

MONEY, SUGAR, ROSES

I worked on *Curious Clover* for three years. It went through numerous drafts, especially as my drawing skills returned to me somewhat. My drawings were all over the place and on my best days, maybe a tiny bit like Glen Baxter's. It was a wildly enjoyable process, and what really took the longest was cleaning the damn thing up in Photoshop. But in the long run none of that mattered, because no one liked it. No one wanted to publish it. No one knew what to make of it. Too much prose to be a comic, too many illustrations to be a novel. Didn't flow like a comic, too much reading etc. And I understood people's criticisms, I really did. I still don't know whether it's actually something kind of cool or just a steaming pile of crap. The thing was: I did it all myself and the world was indifferent.

MONEY, SUGAR, ROSES, CONT.

So I dove back into my day job, and one good thing that happened was I became a part-owner of the store, and was put on salary and was suddenly actually able to afford to live in New York and pay rent and bills on time. Also, in my great antiquity, I discovered internet dating. Sort of.

THERE WAS THIS THING CALLED FRIENDSTER

Long before Facebook. And one of its features was that you could "smile" at someone. The minute that happened, the whole thing turned into a hookup site. In my case, at least. Probably the oddest situation I got into on that front was that two best friends, San Diego transplants, were both "smiling" at me, unbeknownst to each other. One day they're talking about this guy that they're writing with on Friendster, and it turns out it's the same guy: me. They flipped a coin to see who could go on smiling. I was told all this later, in bed, with the one who'd won the coin toss. She also told me she was a virgin. She was twenty-seven and that seemed a little strange so I asked why. "It's a funny story, she said, have you ever seen the movie *Boys Don't Cry*? I was in a situation sort of like that. You know, with a woman pretending to be a man. *And you didn't realize?* Not until later, no, and by then we'd fallen in love."

OH, OH, DIANA

And then I was torn asunder by a woman named Diana.

TEARS

We'd also met on Friendster, and I forsook the former virgin for her. Diana. Who was complicated as a smiling shell, arch and indeterminate, dark and pale and smooth of hair and maidenhair. But quick to judge and take offense, and I was sorry, yes so sorry, every time.

FALL

Lovely Diana moved from Carroll Gardens to "New Victorian Flatbush" while we were together, and it was really dead out there. She was a teacher and a leader of children, but sometimes from that house spoke to me as a child. My fault, really, as I was tired of strangers and dating strangers and all the wind outside and wanted her to be, you know, the final destination . . . So there was the act of the putting upon a pedestal and the lowering of oneself to the level of unworthy, all out of some self-created pressure to make it work.

LIKE

Wandered through her neighborhood, Ditmas Park, one Sunday, through the parlor-warmed and bed-warmed Victorian houses, and everyone was having a yard sale. It was official Yard Sale Day, and it was hot with something snaky in the air. After breakfast we inspected it all. Diana was looking for a bike and I bought some records and old videocassettes. Most of what we thought and felt about each other was being carefully suppressed as we made our way back past the green thresholds of unkempt lawns with garage junk and household bricolage obscuring them.

Someone called my name.

It was J's mother, looking very much unchanged with her gold-red hair and paint-white skin. She was sitting with a small dog, helping out at a friend's yard sale. The scene had a strange lethargy, an idleness to it. I was about to say, "How is J?" Remembering the last time I'd seen him, that strange stoic teenage conversation before the slideshow, like a terminal somehow, before we went off to such different destinations without getting to say goodbye.

But then she said, "You heard what happened to J?"

"No. The last I heard was he got engaged."

She cleared her throat and fixed her sunhat and told me what happened, and when she finished her eyes were moist and glassy, but mine were not because I was in shock, thinking: *One of us has to be strong*. Her garage sale friends were side-shooting me black looks for coming along and making her tell the story and making her cry, so we exchanged emails and I went on my way as quickly as I could.

It was only when I got home from Diana's and those strange, sleepy, waterless gardens where J's mother lived that I could undo my self from myself and cry like I was singing with both eyes closed.

RAIN

On a trip to Stockholm to visit her sister we fell apart. Her family kinda liked me, and she didn't like that. She thought I wasn't transparent enough and must be secretly making fun of them all in my mind. Her sister had had a lovely young baby girl, and I was so moved by the presence of the lovely object of young life that I was inspired to quit smoking, finding that it was somehow a death-scrim between myself and other ornaments of the pink and smooth world of life. Declivities both stern and soft as well: a bicycle ride through the woods, the brother-in-law's awesome Swedish family, swimming with him, Jens, in the lordly cold of that freshwater flasket with plants of the earth all around us and healthy new young pink babies and Swedes. But not enough for Diana. Not I.

OH, OH DIANA

Ended in Iceland on the return, playing pantomime knowing over taking tour trips riding horses swimming blue lagoons sleeping separate beds knowing over making do, separate beds and in the end it all came down to Diana saying I smelled. I smelled somehow like chemicals. "I don't know, it's hard to describe."

3

CHAPTER TWELVE

(lost horizons / coucher et souffler)

Between Diana, *Curious Clover*, and my stolen spy novel lay three things:

One was an off-and-on again affair with a twenty-two-year-old.

Another was Spectacular Bird.

The last was the formulation of a pop philosophy.

And between these three things lay other things: cavernous dark winter times and visits with the family. Fights with co-workers and makings-up.

Then there was a new sponsor, a former adman who taught meditation now, and resonances good and bad such as those that cleft and summit with us in our attempts at normal life-living which is often not easy.

Problems like money. Problems like love. Problems like: Am I alone out here sour and wretched in my desires? For love. For Attention. And on the astral: just by nature a malcontent? All really peachy keen and just can't see?

Thinking: What have you done lately? *Curious Clover* sucked.

Thinking: It was your crappy drawings that ruined it.

Was it disappointment disenchantment disavowal of the notion of art disavowal still with heavy heart thrillers screenplays comics were where the world lay not the old arabesque around your eye or the words that came into your head at night and choked you up like father's razors with their weight and heft and tendered sission.

1) Alexandra
moved and walked through the wink of the world with a little dog named Jasper she'd got to cheer her up after her last suicide attempt. Wampum from her parents after dropping out of Hunter. Parents both therapists, of course, from Northern California. Hairstyle like Bardot but brown, with bangs and a face like Reese Witherspoon with overbite. Only way to tell something wasn't quite right was the cosmic black dusted depths of her eyes. Matchless in sorrow and viceregal with secrets like the moment in early eighties X-Men when Jean Grey boils Mastermind's mind simply by showing him the universe through her eyes.

I said: I can't promise you anything.

She said: It's not like I want to date you or something.

And somehow we wound up fornicating.

It was fantastic.

She had glorious breasts for a girl so slim, and her hair hung down from the brown north like immortal spindles of memory. Alexandra: sunbeams through my Grand Street window highlighting us in our sin, in our trespass against the light. Alexandra: the afternoon hushed in rhythms of rustled blankets and blanketed skin.

Decay and attrition.

Thinking: Haven't I just turned thirty? Shouldn't I be looking for something serious? Trying to settle down: one of those epiphanies evolved on naturally guilty milk brain.

But we would see each other on and off for three or four years, as the blue days fused one to the other and loveless sex became more and more an acceptable thing to me, when loneliness entombed me in its dark and I'd reach for my Motorola.

2) Spectacular Bird
was a band Dave started with a grinning, fantastic bear of a guy named Luis. I joined later. We had all long been into what the record collectors call pop-psych or sunshine pop: bands that had started in the wake of the "Paperback Writer"/"Rain" single. Like: Love, the Zombies, the Left Banke, World of Oz, the Mirage, Honeybus, the End, Koobas, the Common People, Euphoria, Mother Truckers Yellow Duck, the Remains, Donovan, Grapefruit, West Coast Pop Art Experimental Band, Mortimer, the Choir, Cherry People, the Flame, Marmalade, the Idle Race, the Hollies, the Poppy Family, Timebox, Dantalion's Chariot, One in a Million, Wimple Winch, Syn, Tintern Abbey, Blossom Toes, Tomorrow, etc.

That was the sound we aspired to, and we spent a lot of time in the odd house Dave found in Saugerties, practicing and arranging, etc. It was the middle of winter when we actually recorded, and the forest world was ivory with fringes of lacy snow. When the album was done we named it *Emma Lane,* after the street we recorded it on, and threw a party that started fun but grew very dark and strange.

The next morning, twenty or twenty-five of us went to breakfast by Kaaterskill Falls, and then drove back with remorse to the city. Because our sunshine pop was not enough, with its sound-waves and its hopeful ambling towards simple pleasures, to stave off the darkness. Some were, perhaps, momentarily cheered but, that was when I saw: pop is candy, creamy, fruity candy.

It is bright red and melts on your tongue, with no hints of wit or weirdness.

And to get to that point, destination pop, was to give up on this spotlighting of the self, one's own artistic intentions, the notion of an individual "voice." Pop was the thing that flowed and swirled through lagoons of human confusion with good news: the sun is coming and we're going to dance. Or, sexy version: the sun is leaving and we're going to dance.

3) So that was pop.
And I set out, not only with Luis and Dave, but in deeper still unfurling ways of my own, to become it, to breathe it, to let it devour me in its neon pink gums.

Having already embraced the pop poetry of Ian Fleming, the final step was the pop that shone in the pink light of the old cinema palaces in the days before Netflix.

I'd found a Chinese guy named Danny who sold bootlegs near my house, and he was my introduction to the films of Jason Statham and the overall brilliance of Luc Besson's EuropaCorp.

I had made my home in a new and strange land, where the speed of bullets and sarcasm was a momentary salve for the fears, worries, Harper Collins orders I forgot to place, credit cards I forgot to pay, mother's emails I hadn't returned, etc.

With pop in music, film, and words came dreams of mastery. Of *diamond rings* and *things* and *baby you're so cold,* but also the diamond-hard efficiency of the one-man or one-woman army who fought bad guys with phonebooks or watermelons. I looked around at myself and my friends and customers and relations for that kind of mastery, and saw it in only one place: the speed with which they could push the buttons on their computers. And the speed with which their computers could tell them things they no longer needed to remember.

And there it was:

Pop: the bringing of sunshine and smiles, if only temporarily, through the illusory notion of the man-machine, who was really just a stand-in for the speed and efficiency with which their machines operated. Only dreams of super-spy or vampiric invincibility to keep us from the notion of our increasingly snail-like ineptitude.

Pop: machine man, computer, the eventual casings for our delicate and oversized brains.

*****

In the midst of my dopey flirtations with pop, I'd grown obsessed with the Great Game. It was all I read about: Hopkirk. *Tournament of Shadows.* Eventually, a wonderful novel called *The Mandala of Sherlock Holmes* by Tibetan author Jamyang Norbu convinced me to try to do something comics-related with that period so like our own.

Kipling. *Kim.* Kim's game.

Found myself diligently researching. Oracle and empire. Colonial spirit. Mind steps through the imperium of the Afghan desert. Fascinating. Khyber pass. Horrific. This and that Khan playing with the British and the Russians like children.

Anyway, kept researching. Couldn't write. Absolutely no idea where to start. Origins of Jonathan Chase, thinking: Could be cool to have an American in the midst of it all, drifting from scene to scene like a landlocked Huck Finn.

Meanwhile I'd been reading pulp spy novels for years: Nick Carter, Remo Williams, Mack Bolan, the Death Merchant, the Penetrator, Joe Gall. Thinking: Maybe I can't write very well anymore, but perhaps I could write something along those lines? Not realizing: Everyone thinks they can write a thriller.

Pulp aggressor character Jonathan Chase igniting or extinguishing conflicts between empires in the nineteenth century, with perhaps an Indian sidekick? No way, too racist. Perhaps no JC. Perhaps protagonist isn't a white man? Insecurity in a) voicing a character so far removed from me b) details of time period. People are sticklers.

Fuck it.

No go.

*****

Every summer, in lieu of a proper vacation, I'd go to my friend Anne's summer house in New Hampshire. There was a certain order to the process that was pleasing. Daytime: swimming or kayaking in Silver Lake. Naps in the afternoon. Nighttime: taking turns cooking dinner with whoever had come up that year.

The old house was ropey and wooden and bought for a song by a grandfather who'd performed the first ever successful open heart surgery. It had once been a lodge and still held forth with glorious erectness over the mountain with vistas of the lake and Keene.

And through the black knot of nighttime forest, we'd set off fireworks, burn effigies of ourselves and bonfires up into the galaxy.

That was the summer of the conceptual artist.

In an off-time with Alexandra, I was on with the conceptual artist, and we both happened to find ourselves at Anne's that summer. It was the consummation of all things green. Heat, splashes, wagtail hounds all around, phantom motorboats, rhomboid clouds.

Later, at the bookstore near town, I found a box of John Gardner's continuation James Bond novels. Neat embossed covers all, and silhouettes of Bond in triplicate: running, jumping, shooting.

I thought it could be fun to spend the rest of the summer reading them, as I had loved the originals and Kingsley Amis's *Colonel Sun* so much. I had already read and admired Gardner's *The Liquidator*, so I assumed they too would be awesome.

And so it was there, sometime in those hot lake-scented days, up and down the path through the woods, that my Great Game-era notion turned into a Swinging Sixties notion. And perhaps at night, after the conceptual artist, after cloudburst, another kind of transformation took place.

From: I *like* this to I could *use* this.

RUNNING JUMPING
AND SHOOTING

*****

My descent back into full-on plagiarism, and that descent's transformation into something even more egregious, did not all occur that summer. But the notion that these Gardner Bonds were long out of print and perhaps somewhat forgotten was quickly squashed from within by the counter-notion that I really had no idea, after all, who in this world remembered what. Perhaps out there were men who had so loved Gardner's Bonds that they'd memorized every word. How could I ever know?

And then another voice with a certain washed-out pallor: How could I ever know *unless I tried?*

Remembering, however, the sleepless nights and panic attacks earlier days of plagiarism had caused me, I put it out of my head and tried to write a spy novel set in the Sixties on my own. Its hero, Jonathan Chase, was a kind of kung fu master who happened to look like Robert Redford. So, sessile that fall, I played with this character on the page with sentences tumultuously bad and sentences average and otherwise. Query: Why is he a kung fu master? Thoughts about assassins led inevitably to amnesia. To brainwashing. To *The Manchurian Candidate*. To the Korean War. To Vietnam. To Chiun, Remo Williams's Sinanju master. To Jeong, my Chiun rip-off. And therein lay the early days of my spy book.

Sort of a joke. Sort of serious.

Liked the idea, surely, in my conversion to pop, of writing a pulp thriller. Could I actually do it? By then my trust in my own imagination and verbal prowess was as low as it could be without not existing, to say nothing of the rejections of my previous efforts. So no, I did not trust I could really pull it off in a bestseller list kind of way. But perhaps just for me or for friends? To see if I could?

Plugged away with it and plunged my depths – old movies, bad TV – for classic kinds of scenarios . . .

Oh man . . .

just a minute please . . .

sorry . . .

Fuck.

Sorry, this just isn't working.

It's like . . .

It's like the closer I get to the truth, the closer I get to the present day, the harder this gets.

It's Christmas Day today, here on Elba . . .

and . . .

I know it's my fault but I miss the old friends, the old ways, and the old resurrection.

And I know it's my fault, but here in this ocean-green sinner's refuge I miss them.

I miss them all.

Even the ones who mocked and who laughed, and if there is any grace left in this heart or without it let me find it . . .

let it come great thunderhead

oh

fuck

I'm sorry

Just a minute

Okay

you

take

it

from

here

I'm

too

busy

crying.

INTRODUCING!

An Elba Productions
Production

In association with
the producers of Yeti
Publishing
Productions

Featuring the no-good
Plagiarist and the
motions of his mind in
the final chapter of this
memoir . . .

Magic Circles

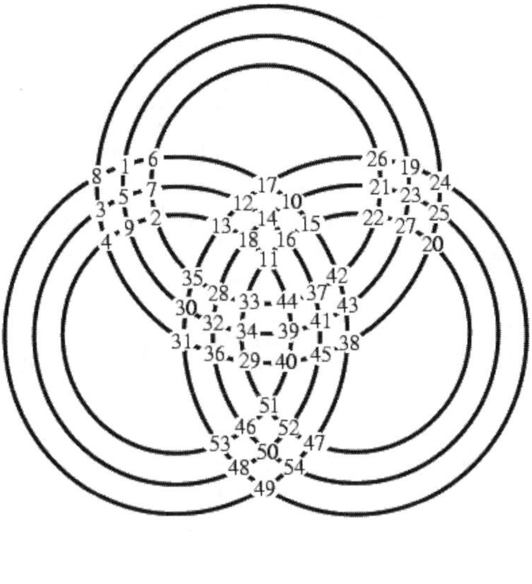

(or the Chapter Thirteen story)

CHAPTER THIRTEEN

(to you who are so few)

I want now to be on the bright side, out in the sun, out of these dark clothes out in the afternoon wilds with you, where everything is a signal and every signal says rolled gold. But I am here still on the other side, the one that is not so bright, writing my history of secret torments and hidden madness and the bogs of my spirit-mind in relation to the western world. Through the open doorway I can see the sun-shadows dancing and the shiver of the children's language and the sound is its own instrument, its own blank canvas, and I want to go sing. But I have not finished my history – my dream history, if you'll humor me – of my own darkness and my own failures and their endless curvilinear repetitions both transparent and semi-transparent and still unknown even to me. It is a double game, this game of post-exilic circumnavigations and ten thousand oscillations to the onion skin called Man; for I find I must be both the fulcrum or trigger and the mirror reflecting it.

Concentric in the nature of circles and the phenomenon of repetition, my mind returns once more to the album *Headquarters* by the Monkees, which I first heard on the twenty-sixth anniversary of my birth at a time when I was trying to step outside of circles and the way they seemed to overlap and redirect. I'd always wanted to hear it because it was the first album on which they played their own instruments and wrote their own songs. It is not nearly as good as the earlier albums with hits by Goffin & King, Nilsson, Boyce & Hart, etc., but it has a certain inaugural character and charm. Because they were, in fact, the Monkees.

Always a source of ridicule for the intelligentsia, people called them names like the Pre-Fab Four, and anti-Monkee sentiment was perhaps as its height just before *Headquarters*. That album's release did help alleviate some of the hatred and unfair targeting, but then the Beatles' *Sgt. Pepper* came out and everyone forgot about lowly old *Headquarters*. No one can deny, however, that in their early days, before the full-on media war destroyed and stripped them of credibility, the Monkees were something special. Something necessary. They fulfilled a role that the market and the net of the market and all the children within that net desired.

And still, somehow: Mickey, Peter, Mike, and Davy managed to maintain a bit of old Benjamin's sense of *aura*.

So let us now follow that all-around net we can't normally see, constructed as it is of liquid solids that, furiously and sometimes fast, melt into air, to the year 2008 or so and the origins of a construct, a pre-fab, a little child born in the ghetto with his head all a-clanging and a-banging against those absence ropes, and let's call him Q. R. Markham.

We were sitting around the kitchen table at my mother's house. My older stepbrother Nick and his lovely

HEY HEY WE'RE THE MONKEES
TRUTH
CRIME
SELF

wife were in town, and I was telling them about a job I'd got writing book reviews and interviewing authors for the *New York Post*. If you know the *Post* at all, you'd be surprised, as I was, to hear it even had a books page. We joked that, because of the politically conservative nature of the rag, I should create a new persona for my reviews. A sort of rough-and-ready type who always wore windbreakers and baseball caps and compared everything he reviewed to the works of Tom Clancy. My stepbrother suggested that instead of stars I could assign each book a number on a kind of Clancymeter.

We all had a good laugh, and ate lunch and they returned home in an aeroplane over silent white sky waves.

Later, when the notion of writing a thriller really took hold in my mind, the valorous figure of the besunglassed and deathless Clancy-man returned. Having studied patterns of success and failure in the arts my entire life, I knew that the truly successful artist or performer in any field is sort of like Christian Bale in *Batman Begins*. He or she must become more than human, a kind of symbol, a legend even. But the creation of that legend, as evidenced by the word symbol in the previous sentence, was once more a kind of language.

With respect to retrospective kinds of dream time: I, as Markham, began adding plagiarized passages to my spy book once I had an agent. I had a good agent. A good man. But a busy man. Who naturally turned me over to someone else. That was David, who I worked with quite a bit in the early stages of the book before it went out.

Once I had an agent, the prospect that this thing, this deformed baby, could really make its way out of the long birth canal and into the world was shocking. Fear returned *cito*. Fear of judgement, of criticism, fear just generally of being observed to exist, I suppose. David suggested I change the prologue, and that's when it all started. Now let me be perfectly clear: that statement does not put any responsibility for my decision on David. All I mean is that, with editing, and the notion of making the work better, all of my old fears of not being good or talented enough returned.

Somewhere between the Clancymeter and the Spenser/Doughty/Green/Updike/Merwin continuum I once favored lay the work of the great Charles McCarry. Born in the Midwest, he'd been a journalist most of his life and worked for the CIA in major hot spots throughout the heights of the Cold War. His experience informed his work in such a way that I believe he and Le Carre are the only spy novelists the real old Cold Warriors take seriously. To me, his prose reads like a less-affected Hemingway, with a more multi-hued understanding of human nature.

I'd been hearing McCarry's name uttered reverentially for many years before I finally came upon a copy of *The Tears of Autumn* at a remaindered book warehouse on a job for the bookstore. I read it in one night and promptly went out to buy the rest of his catalogue.

So when changes were suggested I found my memory creeping back, through the silken doorways and jade scrimmages, to the palace of Mr. McCarry's oeuvre, and I had misdemeanor on my mind. His novel *Second Sight* particularly jibed with what I'd done so far in my stupid old spy book. Having already replaced the prologue with a scene from his *Christopher's Ghosts*, and having thus made the first offense, I went on to change the overall plot of mine from spies being killed all over Europe to spies being kidnapped and brain-drained with a mysterious drug all over the world.

That moment is the moment when I signed my suicide note, so to speak. If *anyone* knew that book. If *anyone* knew that plot, it would be obvious as all hell I'd ripped it off. But denial, never-failing nimble old denial, said to me: There are only so many plots in spy novels. There's a certain interchangeability to them, complex as they are. And new packages are often enough to recontextualize everything for people.

Thinking: McCarry's *Second Sight*, within the context of a more action-packed Eurospy scenario, might not read like McCarry's *Second Sight* at all.

In answer to the obvious question that arrives here: the answer is yes, I knew this was wrong. I knew theft was wrong. But I began to view the sacred rules and immortal codes we use to perceive these kinds of situations as either slightly bendable, slightly permeable, or else as not applying to me. What that says about my moral character I am afraid to know.

And here: I had come to see the publication of my spy book as my last chance after fifteen years of toil, both real and unreal, at any kind of success in the spheres of the literary and the actual.

So: I was willing to bend reality in my mind to see it come to fruition.

Thinking: I would just die if anyone else knew.

But: I know *I* can stand the gradual wearing away of my own conscience if it means not so much literary success as financial success on some level – if I could sell movie rights, perhaps I could actually support a family one day.

David also, wisely, had me remove the more ridiculous kung fu-related aspects of the book. Which, for me, led to a lot more weeding out of my own scenes and the inclusion of a lot more stolen scenes from McCarry and now John Gardner's Bond books.

Thinking about the past in regards to circumambulation or return: we use the phrase "point of no return" to signify the upheaval of the circle, the decimation of the epicenter.

And here it was: magic.

Having altered my plot to follow McCarry's, I now started finding scenes in Gardner's books that – to my simian mind – could greatly improve upon what I had.

A long elevator crashing scene from *For Special Services,* a long chase scene from *Nobody Lives Forever,* an info-dump scene on satellites from *For Special Services,* a local festival chase scene from *License Renewed.* I could go on. But it was in the replacing of my early clumsy work with these fully wrought and masterfully executed action scenes that the book turned into a monster, and at the same time began to feel like something with commercial potential.

Cut to: Faustian bargain.

Days and nights of monotonous criminality retyping passages from these old thrillers into mine. Always had a memory for where a word or passage was, visually speaking, within a book. Easy to go back and find. One new stolen passage sparking off another. Thinking: Villain in *Icebreaker*'s anti-Semitism jibed with the Eye of Gaza leader in McCarry. Making a new composite character from the two. Or, on a more basic note, McCarry's Paul Christopher not carrying a gun fit well with my guy being a kung fu master and using only his fists.

So in this morally downward-tending fashion, I prepared a first draft and sent it to David and waited. There is always a fair amount of waiting with agents. Paradoxical, of course, to realize now that any of those long waiting periods could have been a time to call it off. Find an excuse. Chuck it in the garbage. In the landfill. Or a landfill-flowing ocean. But no: felt unable to surrender to any realization of the truth of my actions, the vastness of my ego, my self-delusion rigid and infallible and penetrative as a circular thing with ten thousand layers of effluvia to it.

In the life I lived on the most auspiciously physical of the ten thousand levels, I had grown reserved and self-possessed. Of course. Had trouble listening to or relating to other people. Formerly things I enjoyed quite a bit as they tended to relax the old tensions, help me let go, care, and *get out of self*. But now I must have appeared to be an unbridled egomaniac. This is in the spring before the summer of 2010, when the book went out.

Most likely: Losing my attention to detail at work, overwhelmed by the drudgery of it, the constant flood of street people wanting money or selling their crappy books or talking about current events as reported in the *Daily News*, I began to appear to some as something of an asshole. I certainly tried to step outside it when I could, to forget it when I could, but it's not so easy to forget the truth. So: all efforts toward avoidance. All efforts toward escape.

Before the book went out on submission but was already hybridized and Frankensteinized, I got into a whole lot of social shilly-shallying, a whole lot of outwardly expressed hithering and thithering as I turned away from the interior. Had a Fourth of July party and made some flirtations with women and just in general tried to walk out with my spirit in the early summertime.

Thinking: Circles, hullaballoo, the occurrence of which didn't necessarily mean the truth wasn't there outside myself, beyond the radius, where, spirit in hand, the world might greet me back. Liar as I was, can't anyone step out in summer to court the world?

A strange side-effect of putting all my energy into denial, to maintain the semblance of a properly socialized individual, was that I started speaking with lots of weird accents.

It was almost as if I only had about twenty-five to thirty percent of my actual self to share with others and so shortcuts were needed even there.

Now I wonder if it didn't appear demented.

Before the days of witch-roasting, however, there were lovely days with a young lady from the West. I only wish I had been more like myself with her. She had that fine flavor of something straight from the earth: tan and lean and curly-headed with good large eyes and a good small button nose. She made wonderful art, wonderfully ahead of her years, and somehow we agreed about everything. She liked all the private press psychedelic and folk I played. The country rock I played. Even the Jesus rock I played. We watched *Claire's Knee* and *La Collectioneuse* and *Pauline at the Beach*, and she loved them. I gave her the books of Rudolph Wurlitzer and she loved them. It was wonderful.

I thought: Life could be this way.

Life could be good.

Life could be good: like the heat of her breath dancing around my face or the soft buttermilk whites of her eyes smiling in the grassy evening, expressive of something non-withering,

everlasting,

blue-blinded,

west-essenced,

summer-lumbery,

star-flowering,

moon-tempered,

sun-gilded,

gold-lettered,

earth-drawn,

and bronze-drawn in its organic circularity, like a counter-clockwise dial attached to my heart. Or: if my heart were a circle of all-embracing nature, perhaps it would meet hers somewhere circumterrestrially and their overlapping would create a new kind of circle of astrological and geometrical goodness.

But then the book sold and I could no longer concentrate on anything else for very long.

It was rejected several upon several times. Most people thought the writing was impressive but had nothing to distinguish it from other spy novels of its kind. There was a certain solemnity to it all, and I thought: Aha, maybe it will sink without a trace and I can still remember part of me hoping for that. Strange to think in such an affirmatively inscrutable situation: the desire for the thing to fail to be the healthy impulse and the desire for it to see light of day the death wish.

We were about to go looking at small presses when David called to say he'd heard from a brand new, not-even-launched imprint at a large publishing house I really admired. They wanted to talk. The next day. He thought I'd probably need to sell it to them a bit, and mentioned they wanted to make some pretty substantial changes.

"That's amazing!" I said to him and to my friends, for part of me wanted just to be able to say at long last, "Look, I have a book deal!" While the rest thought: At the terminus of my success lies destruction. Or: osculation of circles meet here at their consummation where, through re-appropriation, a reciprocation of my errors will no doubt lead to a year's worth of terror and sleepless nights as a kind of reagent.

Thinking: I finally won.

Thinking: I've finally lost.

And when the call was made, in fact there was very little I had to sell. I'd been so worried I'd even asked a very bright British spy novelist named Jeremy I'd been emailing with for advice on how to pitch it to them.

In the end my future editor mostly spoke of how he envisioned the book – when it might come out, what format, etc. – and I told him a little about my ideas for the sequel.

Somehow, *The Day of the Jackal* came up.

And we bonded.

So no definite date at first, but soon: November third, 2011, was put into my mind as the day my life would either begin anew or end entirely.

Right angles, intersection of alpha and beta.

My editor and I had lunch, met, talked, and he was a very cool guy. I was surprised to find he was younger than me and completely dedicated to the thriller in all its forms, though leaning closer to the noir, procedural, and eurocrime side of things than to the world-perambulating superspy.

I was super nervous. He ate dessert.

We went back to the office, also right-angled, glassine, interstices with windows, windows occluding everything, a Parthenon of viewpoints in the delta of midtown.

Later would come the telephone conversation where he gave me, very precisely, a series of major changes to make in the plot. They were good changes that would have, in a different situation, made the book something better and stronger. But this is me we're talking about, dear reader, and by this point you know me well enough to know that is not what happened.

David and, later, my editor both thought they were dealing with someone who was upfront and who he purported to be. Who having already come this far, surely wouldn't have trouble producing more.

But that wasn't me.

And once I'd heard those magic words *change* and *edit* once more, my mind was already peregrinating through the unopened pages of my library looking for scenes that would be appropriate to steal.

That *was* me.

So roughly: I was told in August I'd have to hand in all changes on my spy book in November, and its sequel in December. I took September off work and took a bus upstate with a bag full of spy novels, probably fifteen or so.

Into those honey vestures: I had a little cabin to stay in off Tannery Brook Road and was also allowed to stay with Dave and his amazing girlfriend, somewhere west of there. September felt like summer in those lost estates, mystical with gnats and black streams. But everything outside the boundaries of my skin scene was a blur of green heaven.

Knew it was there. Sometimes the glory. Could touch it and feel it.

But had to keep on.

Finding.

Typing.

Deleting.

Replacing.

Doing what I did.

Strong inclinations to lie out in the sun. To forget. To simply sleep. And I took it all and made it into a goal-oriented thing in my mind. Like my editor was a taskmaster schoolteacher, and I had to just finish these assignments he'd laid out. That way, there was a way for me to stay focused solely on the present – this scene, that scene – and try to forget about the larger equation and the incidental or inevitable meaninglessness of the ordeal.

Almost like one step at a time in reverse.

The secret hidden from myself in the act of busywork.

But the busywork was theft.

He wanted me to cut the middle out of what I had and replace it with a mega sequence, a centerpiece quest. Eventually that became Jonathan breaking into the clinic in Marseilles. That whole sequence, in slightly different form, was in Robert Ludlum's *The Prometheus Deception*. I thought I'd try to read a non-Bourne Ludlum that month, but Ludlum wound up making his way into the book. I imagine if there had been something useful on the back of my cereal box I might have thrown that in as well.

Besides all the outright theft, upstate was fun. We went to an open mic night at some rock'n'roll sushi place and there was this guy Phillip who wore Cosby sweaters and talked like Andre the Giant. He played a lute-like instrument that was really, perhaps, just a stick and a string and he made great pronouncements like, "Uh, oh! Looks like you've got diabetes!"

Later I was told by an earnest townsperson named Journey that Phillip spoke Twilight Speak. It was a kind of language that existed between our world of conscious word usage and that of the spirits, or even the gods.

Each morning I'd return to steal more words.

I quickly had to abandon the idea that Chase could get by without guns. My editor wanted me to put him in a situation where the bad guys had to come to him. This meant killing a Russian and an Englishwoman, an ally, to lure the spies. The amount of killing this new Chase was doing left no other option but for him to get his finger around the trigger of some greasy steel and start blowing naughty motherfuckers away.

While I was making these changes, I was also working on the second book, the one that will go on forever unseen and unmourned into the future's blazing eye.

Spyscraper.

I could talk about it a little, but honestly, what's the point? It was all stolen too: same methods, same authors, same faraway feel in my insides.

Here take it. It's not mine. But it's pretty darn good.

As my tasks began to wane, my conscience throbbed one last time, went unheeded, and died.

But he was slow in dying, old William Wilson, and mostly made it hard to look at the world and love anything about it or even appreciate the harpsichord chords of morning birds and green things going brown and orange and finally taking their leave.

There is that word *fretting.*

Which I like because it makes the act of worrying musical. But my fretting was not soft and syrupy, it was more like the sound of the factory floor, the detonated mine, the giant rock slowly eating the universe.

Purely of interest were its repetitions like car alarms in the night. Humming: *You are fucked.* No I'm not. *They'll figure us out.* No one's gonna care. *Someone will care.* Book will sink without a trace, ninety percent of books do. *Someone!* No one. *Don't you care?* I can live with any amount of internal pain just so long as word doesn't get out. *But why?* Last chance. *Why last chance?* Too old to start again. *But all of life is starting again.* That would require too much humility.

Then all of life with its sky blue eyes will be without you, outside of you, until you can bend, until you can quiver, until you can stop fretting and play the chords.

Start again?

Go on!

Back to town and back to work. I lost my girl from the West. And soon it was Christmas.

Sometimes the glory.

I mucked around with some internet dating, at the suggestion of a friend, but found it to be depressingly lifelike.

Had to make some last-minute changes in January before the book went into production. I was on vacation, but had brought my stash of fifteen books. All very analogue, I suppose.

Every week after that was like a spike on a clock.

Ticking down to November. Taking a little chunk of me each time.

So: next on my list of people to apologize to after David, and then my editor and his boss, are the proofreaders and fact-checkers of the manuscript, as well as the designer of the exterior and interior. He came up with a lovely symbol for the scene breaks.

The page proofs came; the font looked wonderful and we all went over them, even my mother, who caught things no one else did.

Somehow I convinced myself the proofs made it all more legit. That neat font, those page numbers, it had all the semblance of a real book. Wouldn't people mistake it for one?

My editor got blurbs for it from two wonderful thriller writers who were very gracious with their words, and that felt like I'd maybe cleared a certain hoop, if they hadn't noticed anything either. That's the way I began to think about it: as a steady series of obstacles leading to the abrupt sunlight of the final one on November third. Would I still be walking on two feet by then, or would I have slid down into the non-luxurious depths of some shadow somewhere?

And it all happened again across the ocean, with my U.K. publisher and my editor there, who was lovely. She didn't ask me to change a word, being a sort of satellite of the U.S. branch, but there was the same talk of marketing and blurbs and cover images.

So my crime had a kind of carbon copy.

My email correspondent Jeremy was sent an advance copy and blurbed it. It was a wonderful thing for him to do. I was a great admirer of his series and it was very *very* unfair of me to involve him in any of this in any way. I believe that as I had receded from any kind of clear moral viewpoint I stopped seeing people as people. Sort of like in the film of *The Third Man*. The scene on the Ferris wheel in which Holly Martins asks Harry Lyme, "Have you ever seen one of your victims?"

And Harry Lyme points down to the tiny sidewalk people and asks Holly, "Would you really feel any pity if one of those dots stopped moving forever?"

I don't mean to say I had become a mass murderer, only that as long as I was able to maintain a certain level of detachment, I could continue to see people as things.

Useful dots.

And so the long days of waiting began.

Only in sleep was I ever free, when it came, with the dawn just coming, aided by a few Advil PM. Only in sleep could I feel human once more and alive to the beauty and the mercy of the raw life continuum, the flood without secrets.

Sometimes the glory.

I started patronizing Korean massage parlors that offered "full service." They're mostly in midtown, in completely nondescript office buildings where you're buzzed in after you look at a camera. I was fascinated that I was never asked if I was a cop, but perhaps I just don't have that look about me. Anyway, you'd be sort of greeted by an older woman who you'd pay sixty or eighty dollars and then be ushered off to a changing room by a cute Korean woman all in black with rubber boots. You were given a bathrobe and a "table shower" and then taken to a private room. The actual massages were pretty decent and my most vigilant masseuses would comment on how tense I was. And they'd ask questions like "Big handsome man . . . why you not married?" Or "You no have girlfriend?"

I imagine it was all meant to be flattering, but for me it merely drove home the point that, actually, this is about all the relationship I'm capable of right now. And then they'd say, "Oh . . . kay . . . turn over . . . "

And once more I stared into the void.

Back on the street in the city ruin, the livid space of midtown at midday or midnight with its toppling towers and glow lamps and careless whispers, the fear would return, the added shame, and a sense that everyone could see through me.

Through the brightness, the movement and flash, thinking: *They know.*

I told my sponsor about the hand-job parlors, and he said I was a good responsible guy who co-owned a small business and had two books coming out and there was no reason why I couldn't find a more appropriate situation with a mature woman I could actually have a conversation with.

And I thought: He may be giving me a little more credit than is due here, but sure, why not. But the thing that really decided the situation for me was the city of New York.

One evening I climbed the familiar gray stairs of the familiar gray building near the Morgan Library to find a bright yellow, crooked-swinging police line across the door. My favorite place, the one that felt so much like a brothel in Saigon circa 1969, with its garish costumery and thin walls, was gone.

Ratted out to Bloomberg.

Now the void was half mirror.

So I went back on OKStupid with my sponsor's words in hand, and met someone who was, the website told us, a 96% match. And without saying too much, I'll just say I wish I could have spared her what happened later. But of course I couldn't tell her, couldn't warn her. I hadn't even told my therapist. Or my sponsor. And the thing is, we really liked each other, and eventually came to love each other as the days hummed away in their breathless way. But I should never have been involved with someone, knowing, in whatever capacity, what might or what would happen.

We just sort of melted together, the two of us, it was so easy and so simple, and in the early days, before the pre-publication stuff ramped up, it was easy to forget there was a book at all, entranced as I was by her and her hilarious dogs. Wonderful jerky dancing dogs who loved her so much they really did dance when she came home. One was a rescue, who'd been a stud dog and lived his life in a cage and never really learned how to be a proper dog. He rarely barked, but made rather freakishly Ewok-like vocalizations. The other was a Boston terrier, who pinned me down and licked me into submission whenever she could and sat on top of me to signify to all that I was her property.

That summer we went once more to Anne's. That summer of spearmint and scarlet and bluebottles and the lime of the lake. We took one of the dogs out on a kayak and went to a drive-in movie and it was all *dolce far niente*.

I was still a human being then, in the basic sense of the term, and perhaps could still have stopped the November clockwork, but thought it too far gone.

So I floated out to sea in my floaty donut, into the

sun flare and sea flare with a floaty donut into the night stalks and anemones: mysterious, narcotic, soporific, the perfumed lake, anemone sea, linked together in the ash grasses and night stalks and dank flutters and froths of lazy white air.

Goodbye to the clockwork.

I set it in motion.

Goodbye to the crimson city.

City of your birth.

Goodbye to the whispering wickedness of all I had been.

Your blatant imitation.

Goodbye to the heavenly host of the word, my once and ever lord.

Without any hope of reformation.

Unroll me now like a ball of string.

So that we shall know all your secrets.

Unroll me now, brave souls of the white and pink lemon papers.

So that we shall at once divine all your secrets.

Unroll me now, brave souls of the languid circuitry connected as you are, so limply.

So that we shall see with our own eyes all your secrets.

Yes! For I was once an assassin of that word.

And I was once, once, and once an assassin of that word.

And here you are, once more back to town, another summer ended like a silk hat fallen in a pile of turds. Once more back to work. The street people had been waiting for you. So and so has a new radio. The "neuroscientist" is just not making do without you. How dare you go away? They needed you: for spare change, therapy, and to assuage that old cold feel of aloneness. I know it, I do. And that's why I always tried to be nice. But your co-workers were worried. Thought it had all gone to your head. Neglecting your duties. Book got picked up by the Book of the Month Club and was up for a prize and there were murmurings of good reviews with a month or so to go. So the stakes were higher and kept rising. Girlfriend found a place in the neighborhood I liked. Expensive, but perfect. There was an offer for a ghostwriting thing. Would help pay. Everything on my end, obviously, predicated on an empty core. She didn't know, too late to tell her, only way I thought was to just go through the eternum continuum and on the other side perhaps you'd still float. So the clockwork tightened. We got the place. It was the dream place and Hollywood called and I talked to Hollywood from the bookstore while ringing up customers and we both agreed on which actor should play Chase and who should write the screenplay and the date was now set for the book launch party and then I'd move in with her a few days later.

The good people at my publisher put me on a night at the mystery bookstore downtown with the grand wizard and two great writers, and we did questions and answers. I signed my name as Q.R. Markham and I was out in the world.

And the noose was tightening.

The John Gardner Bonds I'd stolen from had just been re-issued and were there in the window of the mystery store, with introductions by its owner. Let the circle be unbroken. Same owner had blurbed Charles McCarry many times. If he read my book, well, forget it.

Sure I'd lied and cheated and acted before, but this

was a new sort of act, more like a tightrope act where any little misstep or slip of the tongue could bring the house down, raw, red, and bloody dead.

Next night, November third, the actual release date of the book was my girlfriend's birthday. We had an early dinner and took the dogs to their new house. We woke up early to go to Ikea for something, and she got mad at me for not being helpful enough, or not interested enough. I seemed spaced out and I apologized and said I'd be fine after the book release party that night.

The party was fun even if I was all ambulance ears all the time. My lovely publicist and marketing director were there, and my editor gave a little introduction when I read, and the atmosphere was friendly and fun and my heart broke at the outpouring of friends I hadn't seen in years. And, unlike two nights before at the mystery bookstore, I did it all without flinching or feeling as though I was acting. The truth felt so far buried there, among friends, that the reading was about as performative as going to visit a grandparent. There are just certain things you don't bring up.

I can remember going to our new place that night and thinking: Wow, this is my new life. So good. So easy. And when she fell asleep the night thoughts came, with their gold embrace and the hurtness of the hurt. And I tried to do some self-will smoothing over but it was a big one. This was the big one. The book existed now, in more than just my mind.

Anyone could pick it up at any time and admonish me.

I suppose you could say I was tense.

That of course would be a statement with a slightly

suppressed truth to it. And suppression was something I was undeniably talented at.

But it had to come out somewhere, didn't it?

So the weekend passed and I can't remember a thing about it. Monday came and Dave and his girlfriend were playing a show at Zebulon and I tried to rush down there to see them. Just minutes before, however, I had tried to post something on Jeremy's Facebook page only to find he had defriended me.

As I closed up the bookshop my heart began to race. Thinking: Perhaps he'd noticed something stolen in the interview we'd done together for my British publisher? Or in the post I'd done for his website?

I missed Dave's band but I hung out with him and some other old friends for a while. Strangely, the crowd that night included all kinds of faces I hadn't seen around town since the late '90s. But I was too preoccupied for it to be a real hang. My mind was on the internet and I rushed home.

No emails. No news. Just one de-friending.

Fear now upward-curving, I didn't sleep. Just lay there with my laptop on my chest sort of waiting for something bad to happen, but at the same time didn't allow myself to expect the worst.

Dawn came like a glow lamp and the morning was tranquil. I dozed off for an hour or so and slept through the first phone call.

Brightness. Forms taking shape. Telephone ring.

It was the bookstore. They said, "Call your agent."

I checked: missed calls from my agent.

Thinking: Now is the time of the misty eyes and the merciless beat of my own heart that I know is fear.

Thinking: Now is the time before the truth, before the mocking lightness comes trembling through. Thinking: Now is the time.

And before I could dial him, my phone rang.

"I just got a very disturbing phone call."

"Really?"

"Yeah . . . do you . . . do you know who Jeremy is?'

"Y . . . "

"Well he's made some very disturbing accusations that there's passages in your book . . . from Ian Fleming and . . . Geoffrey O'Brien . . . "

"Okay . . . "

"We have a conference call with them in five minutes."

"Okay."

"Okay."

So.

Five.

Minutes.

I had come to the edge of my window, to the sill, and looked out at the street below that I had looked at so many times in dusk and night and other blue times. Thinking: Was this the street on which I was meant to die? Was this the wild, abandoned moment in which I was meant to take flight? Was it as simple as a running jump, a sweep through the heavy air, cresting the wind to fall aglitter with morning flesh and spouting blood, blood in waves, and once more with them, downward, doubled, among the frozen and the dead in the white morning time?

In the white time.

Thinking: Carcass in the road.

Remembering: My aunt, a woman very dear to me, jumped out her window when my uncle died. Then my cousin, her daughter, blaming herself, also committed suicide. So my cousin Steve lost his whole family in the course of a year.

Remembering, as a child: Asking my mother what she would do if I died. And she said: I would kill myself. Thinking: I cannot be responsible for the death of another person on this earth.

I may have grown up *wrong* or just backwards to the cataract roar of the waterfall and the unbeheld orbit of planets and all the things people do who live without shame in endless perfection, but I could not see another person die for me, because I don't deserve that. I do not believe in violence. I do not believe in anger. I do not believe in hurt. I have pointed all of those things towards myself all my life and endlessly like a weapon, but I could never hurt another living thing on purpose. I could never willingly allow another life to end except my own, and even that I have clung to sometimes, like a lover.

And then my five minutes was up.

I dialed the conference call number.

"Hi, it's Quentin."

All went quiet on the line.

Someone's voice: "Quentin, certain accusations have been made regarding . . . "

"It's true."

" . . . "

"It's all true."

Silence.

"I'm sorry. It's all true."

"Quentin, thank you for being so upfront about the matter. I am going to turn you over to our publicity director . . . "

"Quentin?

"Hi."

"Quentin, we're going to issue a press release in an hour. Just make sure you don't say anything to anyone. Okay?"

"Okay."

"They'll come on strong for a while but it will pass. Just don't say anything and if you have any questions call me . . . "

"Okay."

Click.

Oh click.

Oh shit.

Oh motherfucking shit.

With the whipping post in sight, there was suddenly this tremendous déjà vu. As if I had at last completed the requirements of a cycle and was beginning a new one. Either way, it was gone.

That great and solid weight of duplicity that I'd worn like a millstone around my neck since college. So hard to write about, isn't it, the truth? It's a transfiguring thing for sure, to step out of the unsavory light of a lifetime of lying and be able to cry.

Mostly with relief that I could finally stop. That I could stop plagiarizing. That I could stop everything insomuch as plagiarism had become a sort of stand-in for control, for self-will, perhaps even a way of getting back at the world. So I cried, but it was with happiness and relief for all of the good things that could come from no longer having any secrets. I was tired and unbalanced with the sun in my eyes, and the world seemed in that moment like a place of great tenderness.

But it dawned on me quickly that what for me was the end of a years-long chamber of subterfuge would be brand new to everyone else. And that they would most certainly *not* share my sense of relief in finally confessing my vicissitudes and having a sort of dissecting spotlight shone on my innards.

No doubt I was also in shock because I called work first, told them everything, but said I'd still be in at four, no problem. I spoke to my father after that, who was quite clearly shocked but pragmatic, and without circumspection understanding, and offered to come and stay with me immediately. But I declined and then called my mother, who wasn't home. So I called my girlfriend and she said come over and I told her about it and we napped or tried to nap, but I kept realizing that nothing was the same. As normal as the day was, before the phonecalls came, it still felt like I'd stepped out of one mystery and into another.

And these moments would come and come again like phantoms, revelations of absolute and everlasting change. Though nothing had changed physically in my world, I had walked through some interstellar juncture into a new one. Certain rights and privileges of the private individual were no longer mine.

The phone began to ring, but I preserved silence. I'd listen to the messages, and the reporters were all very friendly. Just wanted to talk off the record, or we had this and that mutual friend. And it was tempting, so tempting, as I felt I had been unburdened, to want to speak the truth, to go back to the very beginning and explain. But I had speedily found with my girlfriend and father and co-workers that my pronouncements and prognostications were not being fully understood or absorbed because of the, well, the absolute insanity of the thing I'd done.

For them, no doubt, it was like friend or lover turning to them and saying, "So I burned down a school yesterday. But the good thing is I'm completely over it! And I'm willing to admit it all now!"

Putting myself in their position, I realized I was being perhaps overweening in my attempts to emphasize the overall future benefits of the situation. Trying to slow the old whirligig down, I settled in, prepared to answer questions and wrote an email to close friends explaining it all as best I could.

My father called to check in and told me there was a website up with the headline: *Q.R. Markham, Plagiarist.* So there it was, that word. Latin: kidnapper. *Plaga*: net. I always looked at it and thought *Plagia,* like *La Plage* or *Playa Blanca.* But I'd certainly never seen it, evil-denoting and eighteenth-century-rooted as it was, so close to my name or pen name.

My real name was quickly revealed. And other dark places were also quickly revealed as the light of the truth, not my truth, but a truth radiated whisperingly over myself and my loved ones. In this endeavor, the instrument of technology was used as an extension of people's overtaxed fingertip-minds, until the softest, most downy of flesh was found. And once it was found, the site of the wound determined, penetration was made with great clinical objectivity. The wound was opened, at first tenderly, by wound-fanciers, but others arrived at the site and seeing the blood and the skin, pierced already as it was, decided they could fit in there. Could penetrate a little bit. Just for the good and upright purpose of information technology and the fingertip/brain extension.

The raking of the hopeless one had begun. They had come with their ever-changing harpoons and the headless face of Tradition on their sides.

Whisper.

I was young once.

Precocious.

Sorry.

And to the sound of a thousand fingers tapping, rope-noosed, around the world, I said to my girlfriend, to everyone, "You shouldn't be around me now. I am a target. I can withstand any amount of pain but you don't deserve to and shouldn't have to. So I will just go."

And as the unwinding of the onion increased, restitution was demanded, reparations commanded in the valley of the town square.

But I was sworn to silence.

And the gutter punks from the gutter press were coming back with their cattle prods and their microscopes.

Thinking: If I talk I get sued?

Thinking: If I don't talk they continue to regard me as, what? The devil's toilet?

But I knew there was no kind of loss I didn't deserve.

It was the hardest with my mother because it was all for her, really. Everything I'd ever done in this life had involved a kind of squirming to impress her. To say: *Look! I'm worth it!* And to suddenly be none of the things, in the creative sense, she thought me to be, was the hardest part for me in it all. The sense of having failed her.

When I'd been younger I'd been able to live off the

luster in her eyes when I'd done something that pleased her.

Those were the happiness times.

The achievement of something laudable in the eyes of my mother. And over the years, the incentive to live in the luster of her eyes was always there and never felt like extravagance; even as I grew older and still had no money or children, the plenitude of my creative gifts and the constant resonance of new projects in the works always seemed to cheer her.

But to say at last: Mother, I am nothing, I have done nothing, I have been nothing, was the act that finally destroyed me.

Dear Quentin, have you seen this article in which the author describes you as a weasel and a jackass and concludes you ought to be run over by a truck?

Yes. Thanks, Mom. That's a good one.

The intelligentsia of the world had spoken. With all the earth-trembling power and gravitas of the Old Testament patriarchs. Only today's bombardiers of tongue and pen and Twitter preferred words like *douchebag.*

Face burning red and corrupt, I turned the other cheek to say hello to my movers as they carried away my book collection and my furniture. And when that was done, I slept on a floor for a while and went out to meetings several times a day and spoke to lots of friends.

I drafted and sent apologies to all parties involved in my deception: the plagiarized authors, my editor, agent, the writers who blurbed the book, the literary estates. And I am sorry that some of those people found them insincere. But how *can* a person really show how sorry they are? I just wonder, because I would have done it.

Had I been able to see these individuals as more than abstractions, I could never have done what I did. And in the end, it was Harry Lyme in *The Third Man* who helped me to understand the furor and coal-raking *I* was experiencing: *I* was an abstraction to them and therefore just as easily tarnished.

They could not see me crying in the morning's faint light, or saying my goodbyes to floats of friends who knew me and loved me for me, as I loved them in return for their heaven-met and ipsorelative individuality.

They could not see me shambling about with nervous tension, throwing up every few minutes or walking through the former sites of my life like a stranger, like Wakefield in the Hawthorne story.

They could not see me trying to explain what had happened to my friend who worked at the corner deli, who had seen me in the paper and asked if you had to pay to get in there? Or the wagging tails and crystal eyes of the little dogs as I said goodbye.

They could not see me packing my two bags and leaving for the airport with my mother like twin tigers in the night, under the velveteen half-moon and the weight of fifteen wasted years saying *I am so sorry to you* mother

and *I am so sorry* to you father *I am so sorry to you* Joe and *so sorry to you* Anna and *so sorry to you* Nick and *so sorry to you* Yas and *so sorry to you* Rachel and *so sorry to you* Steve and *so sorry to you* Joan and *so sorry to you* Lou and *so sorry to you* Betty and *so sorry to you* Lansing and *so sorry to you* Whitney and *so sorry to you* Kingsley and *so sorry to you* K.J. and *so sorry to you* Amity and *so sorry to you* Paul and *so sorry to you* Brad and *so sorry to you* Marianne and *so sorry to you* Antonia and *sorry to you*

Nora and *so sorry to you* John and *so sorry to you* Miriam and *so sorry to you* Wes and *so sorry to you* Theresa and *so sorry to you* Michael and *so sorry to you* Jeremy and *so sorry to you* Ruth and *so sorry to you* Duane and *so sorry to you* Greg and *so sorry to you* David and *so sorry to you* other David and *so sorry to you* Edward and *so sorry to you* Sarah and *so sorry to you Simon* and *so sorry to you Chauncey* and *so sorry to you* Curious and *so sorry to you* Charles and *so sorry to you* John and *so sorry to you* Elleston and *so sorry to you* David and *so sorry to you* Daniel and *so sorry to you* Geoffrey *and so sorry to you* Robert and *so sorry to you* Richard and *so sorry to you* Janet and *so sorry to you* Howard *and so sorry to you* Stephen and *so sorry to you* Captain and *so sorry to you* Jean and *so sorry to you* Graham and *so sorry to you* George and *so sorry to you* Brigid and *so sorry to you* Steve and *so sorry to you* Fiona and *so sorry to you* Fred and *so sorry to you* Joe and *so sorry to you* Miles and *so sorry to you* Jonas and *so sorry to you* Susan and *so sorry to you* Rachel *and so sorry to you* Jamie and *so sorry to you* Claire and *so sorry to you* Kate and *so sorry to you* Sean and *so sorry to you* Fred and *so sorry to you* Brandon and *so sorry to you* Carol and *so sorry to you* Susan and *so sorry to you* David and *so sorry to you* Zach and *so sorry to you* Lauren and *so sorry to you* Alex and so *sorry to you* Dylan and *so sorry to you* Mary and *so sorry to you* Bill and *so sorry to you* Ken and so *sorry to you* Ariel and *so sorry to you* Charles and *so sorry to you* Monica and *so sorry to you* Anne and *so sorry to you* Sam *and so sorry to you* Michal and *so sorry to you* Rose and *so sorry to you* Suzy and *so sorry to you* Hannah and *so sorry to you other* Hannah and *so sorry to you* Maura and *so sorry to you* Katherine and *so sorry to you Lisa* and *so sorry to you* Bridget and *so sorry to you* Besa and *so sorry to you* Janet and *so sorry to you* Lindsey *and so sorry to you* Jane and so *sorry to you* Nicole and *so sorry to you* Diana and *so sorry to you* Erin and *so sorry to you* Sarah and *so sorry to you* Tianna and *so sorry to you* Lexi and *so sorry to you* Sarah and *so sorry to you* Blossom and *so sorry to you* Mary and *so sorry to you* Melissa and *so sorry to you* Hillary and *so sorry to you* Pelin and *so sorry to you* Jennifer and *so sorry to you* Andrea and *so sorry to you* Jessica and *so sorry to you* Barbara and *so sorry to you* Courtney and *so sorry to you* Brynn and *so sorry to you* Miriam and *so sorry to you* Dave and *so sorry to you* Andy and so sorry to *you*

whose body is its own atmosphere and whose mind is still free and far from the forbidden tree

Dear J:

Today the skyline here on Elba drones with grasshoppers and wood shadows, and they let me out to take a walk when the shafts of evening came like milk-fingers through the bars of my digs. I set out down the old unclean road that leads to the big hole, coloring my thoughts faintly with memories of the two of us in our school days and tennis shoes. I don't want you to think I've forgotten anything when it comes to you, but the messengers from that other world, with their strange gowns and garments, keep telling me I have to write my own story, not yours, if I ever want to leave this vague place. They say I have three weeks, just until the third of January, if I want these words to see the light of day in the fall.

Every boy sooner or later . . . must put away his toys and become a man! *Do you remember that line, J? From* Spider-Man #50? *It's the issue called "Spider-Man No More," in which Peter Parker quits being Spider-Man to devote more time to his studies and to Aunt May. He's grown tired of getting so little respect from the sore people of New York: bystanders are booing him at crime scenes and J. Jonah Jameson has started up a new smear campaign, delivering anti-Spider-Man rants on TV.*

So he throws his bright costume into a garbage can and walks away through the barren wastes of a dead alley in a dead land, and the city loses a hero. Peter Parker walks into a new and sunken world of desolation while all around the city realizes – as the poison queue of crime wave after crime wave shuffles in – how much they needed him. They just couldn't bear it. The captivity of their weakness and their overall lack of power. They couldn't stand the notion that they needed someone to brighten their footpaths with beauty and goodness.

So the phalanx of them badmouthed him and spat at him and came to consider his a diseased personality until he, who had never been concerned with abstractions like power, walked away and left the brawling herd of them to rot in their gray city death-cunt of destruction and savagery.

I have at last tossed away my toys without so much as a backward eye and, leaving this alley now and out into the twilight yellow, I have found a new distraction. It is a giant hole dug in the ground here on Elba, too steep to try and caper down. It's really very deep, J, deeper than you or I or any one man could dig. But I understand they are militant here, and vigilant too, when it comes to such things, and never waver.

So the hole was dug by men, and it was dug well.

It's become a kind of routine for me, after a day of writing in my notebooks to wander down here and stare into it. I see mud and I see rock and the rill of rocks, the spur of rocks over gray pools of water at the grasp of its black base. Sometimes there are men down there, workers, bucking around like mountain goats.

Sometimes they call up to me: "How is your shame coming along?"

Or: "You're one of the child dictators, right?"

And: "Remember, the shame is real. The shame means you are getting better. You are allowing Elba to do its work. Follow the shame."

They are right. Shame has been perfecting its reign here on Elba for so long, epochs now. "Don't look too deep, though," they tell me. "Don't look too deep if you want the truth. Because it has nothing to do with history."

There is the quality of the ruin about their hole, even though it's all quite new and I find it easy to lose myself in thought staring down into the reluctant silence and ruin of this scrappy underworld place.

Once I heard a song by Paul McCartney about fixing a hole. It's on the album that made everyone forget about Headquarters. *People presumed it was about heroin because of the word fix. McCartney was never a heroin user as far as I know, though Lennon was certainly there at the end, when they broke up the band.*

Before I came out here, J, people were saying I looked like Lennon. Like a fat version of him. More recently, someone said I was actually fat Chapman. You know, Lennon's killer.

You and I both know that I have never been a violent man, nor a willfully hurtful one. And the Great Ghost Man in the Sky (that some call Him and some call Her) knows I've made mistakes, big mistakes, but never malicious ones, certainly not violent ones. And as you know, Lennon has always been one of my heroes. For me he stands with gaitered feet on a perch next to Spider-Man, James Bond, and Mountain Dew. Being compared to his killer, being compared to the perpetrator of any crime other than taking other people's words and rearranging them, was confusing to me.

The hole has helped with that. I come and stare down into it, the scallop of its hollow shell and dead earth, and I am able to think once more undisturbed. Sometimes when I look down into its silver and blue sconces, I realize I am now resigned to be flipping burgers for the new mystics, the new visionaries of our time: the businessmen, media types, and web designers.

And even though I can't whistle, I'll whistle anyway, that song "Fixing a Hole." I do it to remind myself about beauty, because I fear that some will begin to find a kind of beauty in the hole itself soon.

It is going to be the hub of a network of light commuter trains, they say. And as the wind blows sweetly upon its cakey human dirt, I think once more of you. The great irony is that you, who were so vibrant, died so young while I who have always worn around me a kind of death in life, may now live to be old here.

You had just married and had the rest of your life before you when you started having trouble breathing on your honeymoon and found out quickly the cancer had overtaken your lungs. You died a young man, on a white bed, in a silver-frosted hospital room, quietly inhaling your last breaths from the fabric of the air.

I myself smoked cigarettes for years and my lungs seem to be fine.

But for what? What great accomplishments can I look forward to now? What great loves? What great works of art?

All I have now, besides my hole, is this manuscript.

In the wake of the uproar about my supposed "confession" on a website called "The Fix," I thought perhaps I ought to write a real one, on a slightly grander scale. But this time with feeling, as they say. And though I only had a few weeks to make it in, I thought I'd make it to you.

So here it is, my confession: told in concentric circles of gradual abasement not in the hope of placation or commensuration, but merely as a once-and-for-all meditation on what I did and what I thought in those years when I struggled with the light, of love and reality, not because I feared the malignant convolutions of death by suicide and the wrath of the One True Ghost Man in the Sky, but rather because, young Jonathan Slemmer, my oldest and best friend, I never got to say goodbye.

Elba,
Nov-Dec 2011

ACKNOWLEDGMENTS

The author wishes to thank Mike McGonigal and Steve Connell for taking a chance on him, Mairead Case for whipping him into shape, Susan Willmarth for being a champion, Rachel Day for knocking it out of the park, Josh Bayer for his fine draftsmanship, Kevin Shields for his title, Lou Rowan and Stephanie Rauschenbusch for early readings, Andrea Auge, Barbara Slemmer, Gus Powell, and the good people of Brooklyn Quaker Meeting.